27 Mixers Jailed On Arrival Here

Arrests Made Quietly; Trial Is Set Friday

UNLOADING IN JACKSON — Negro members of bi-racial group calling themselves "freedom riders" climb out of bus at Trailways Station here early Wednesday afternoon. National Guardsmen with rifles and bayonets are visible in background. — Photo by Nations.

By WALLACE DABBS
Clarion-Ledger Staff Writer

Trial for 27 so-called "freedom riders" arrested here Wednesday when they arrived at the Trailways bus station, has been tentatively set for 4 p.m. Friday in Municipal Court.

Chief of Detectives M. B. Pierce said the integrated group will be tried for refusing to obey an officer and committing a breach of the peace.

City Prosecutor Jack Travis said if they were found guilty, they would receive up to six months in jail and fined $500.

James Farmer, national director of the Congress of Racial Equality (CORE) was among those arrested.

No attempt has been made to post bond which has been set at $500 on each charge, Travis said.

COLLEGE STUDENTS

The group, composed mostly of college students, was divided into two travelling squads on the trip from Montgomery. The first bus-load arrived in Jackson early Wednesday afternoon.

Officers arrested the nine Negro men, one white man and two Negro women as they entered the bus terminal white waiting room.

Twice officers ordered the group to move out and twice the order was refused. They were placed under arrest and hustled into a patrol wagon for the trip to the city jail, two blocks away.

"We are not going to let anyone come into Jackson and openly violate our laws," Chief Pierce said. "Any such group or persons will be dealt with accordingly," he said.

A second bus carrying 15 riders arrived in Jackson at 4:45 p.m. They were arrested after refusing to move on when ordered by officers and taken to jail.

The arrival of the much publicized group which has hoped to break Mississippi segregation laws, was without the violence which rocked Montgomery when they arrived in that Alabama city Saturday.

Passers-by milled around the bus terminal but there were no incidents and the crowd dispersed when the patrol wagon hauled the group away. Police remained in the area, directing traffic.

PIERCE APPRECIATIVE

Chief Pierce expressed appreciation for the lack of violence and

OVER   Continued On Page 2
ON BACK OF PAGE

GOVERNOR EXPRESSES HIS THANKS

Governor Ross Barnett was happy Wednesday night that events of the day had come and gone without untoward incident. He said he was elated with state and local authorities' work in the handling of the trip to the state of the so-called "freedom riders."

His appreciation went also to "all citizens of Mississippi for their splendid cooperation, and for permitting the officers to handle the situation," he said.

Clarion Ledger
May 25, 1961

FROM CALIFORNIA TO A MISSISSIPPI JAIL—Pictured abov
is a group of California students who paused briefly las
Friday evening in Los Angeles while enroute on a Free
dom Ride from Berkeley, Calif., to Jackson, Miss. Fron
row, from left to right, are: Thomas Roland, Father Gran
H. Muse, Jr., Joan Pleune, Jorgia Siegel, Rita Carter, Les

...ra Peterson and Peggy Kerr. Rear are: William Waggoner, ...red Muntean, Richard Thorne, Robert Martinson, Duncan McConnell, Joe Pratt and Lawrence Triss, Jr. They were immediately arrested Tuesday upon arrival in Jackson, Miss.

PAGE 1 Portion of the front page of the *Clarion-Ledger* on May 25, 1961, the day after the first Freedom Riders came to Jackson. Clipped and filed by the State Sovereignty Commission.

PAGES 2-3 Photograph from the *Los Angeles Sentinel*; this group was arrested on June 20 at the train station.

PAGES 4-5 The first bus of Freedom Riders arriving on May 24.

PAGES 6-7 Doris Castle being shown the way at the Greyhound station, May 24.

PAGES 8-9 Albert Dunn being frisked at the Trailways station, May 28.

PAGES 10-11 Gwendolyn Jenkins with police at the airport, June 7.

ABOVE *From left to right:* Price Chatham, Kenneth Shilman, Joe McDonald, Ruby Doris Smith, Charles Butler, and Joy Reagon in a paddy wagon after their arrest at the Trailways station on June 2.

BREACH OF PEACE

PORTRAITS OF THE
1961 MISSISSIPPI FREEDOM RIDERS

ERIC ETHERIDGE

PREFACE BY ROGER WILKINS   FOREWORD BY DIANE MCWHORTER

ATLAS & CO.
NEW YORK

GO GREYHOUND

Out-of-state Freedom Riders rode Greyhound and Trailways buses from
Montgomery and Nashville to Jackson, and were arrested on charges of
"breach of the peace" when they integrated the white and "colored" waiting
rooms, restrooms, and restaurants at the stations on arrival. Local Riders
were arrested when they integrated these same facilities and tried to buy
tickets on departing buses. The Trailways station has since been torn down.
A local architect preserved the Greyhound station, converting its interior
for use as his firm's office. Photographed July 23, 2006.

PREFACE

ROGER WILKINS

By the time the Freedom Rides began in May 1961, the nation's awareness of the system of racism in the South had risen markedly. It had been seven years since the Supreme Court decision in *Brown* vs. *Board of Education*.

Shortly after the decision came down, there was the Montgomery Bus Boycott, then nationwide sit-ins by black college students and flares of violent resistance to court orders to desegregate schools across the nation, particularly at Little Rock Central High School. But nothing struck the consciousness of the country harder than the Freedom Rides.

Blacks in the South knew all about the unforgiving brutality of the enforcers for the segregationist regime. Northern blacks had carefully stored family memories. Their nighttime recollections served as a cautionary tale to younger innocents who were venturing south for the first time. In my family, it was the story of my paternal grandparents being run out of Mississippi by the threat of lynching. My grandfather had successfully defended himself against an assault by a white man intent on enforcing the white privilege of beating a black showing insufficient humility. Few Northern white people carried such graphic lessons about how white supremacy was really enforced in the South.

Segregation was the lasting humiliation thrown up by the enormous backlash mounted by Southern whites against blacks and white Northern "carpetbaggers" at the end of Reconstruction. Outraged at blacks participating in politics, serving in high office, and participating in law enforcement, the white South struck back with a vengeance. A reign of terror ensued, carried out by such vigilante groups as the Ku Klux Klan and the Knights of the White Camelia. Blacks also knew that in many places Southern white law enforcement was often intermingled with, and undistinguishable from, these anti-black terrorist organizations, or from plain old racist thugs.

The central project was to keep uppity, usurping blacks in their place. The violence and terror employed by some white Southerners in the mid-twentieth century was a modern version of the disabling of blacks that harked back about 280 years—to the period when Virginians chose black slavery as the prime source of labor for their economy. By 1700, Robert "King" Carter, the largest slaveowner in Virginia, had developed the practice of "seasoning" new slaves who appeared not to grasp their status as sub-human tools whose only purpose was to serve will of the master. A finger, an ear, or a toe was lopped off the apparently prideful slave. The wound served as a reminder to the offender and to all other slaves who saw her that they should not dare dream of expressing a will of their own.

Brutal subordination of the slaves was also a central tactic in controlling low-status whites who, if not thrown the bone of white supremacy, might have questioned the vastly unequal distribution of wealth and power among whites, which

Southern grandees enjoyed and protected with guile and force.

That regime was still firmly in place at the beginning of the twentieth century, as evidenced by the declarations of two significant Southern leaders of the time. In a speech to the Southern Education Association in 1900, Paul B. Barringer, the chairman of the faculty at the University of Virginia, said that a black should be given nothing more than "Sunday School training" since his principal function in life was to be a splendid "source of cheap labor for so warm a climate; everywhere else he is a foreordained failure, and as he knows this, he despises his own color."

Three years later, Senator "Pitchfork Ben" Tillman of South Carolina took to the floor of the United States Senate to excoriate President Theodore Roosevelt for having Booker T. Washington as a guest for a meal at the White House. "Because of what Roosevelt has done," Tillman fulminated, "we will have to kill a thousand niggers to put them back in their place." The theory was that if threats, economic oppression, and political neutering didn't work, denial of education and brute force had to be used to reassure lower-class whites that their central psychological prop in a hardscrabble world—their superiority over black people in all realms of life—would be protected at all costs.

Segregation was a never-ending, all-encompassing cultural and economic battering of the souls of the victims—relegated as they were to the leftovers of America's growing wealth through the first half of the twentieth century. The culture taught us that all power was held by white men and all beauty was possessed by white women. All the good things—playing major league baseball; teaching and learning in prestigious universities; getting your name praised in the paper (rather than being denounced as a criminal); living in a good part of town rather than the worst; being judged by police as a decent citizen rather than a potential threat; and having access to good white-collar jobs with pathways to the top, rather than the worst jobs with very low ceilings—were in view, but out of reach.

In the North, blacks were largely ignored or rendered invisible in menial jobs. Police forces whacked black heads in the ghetto when it was deemed necessary to keep the established order intact. In the South, as the country passed mid-century, the Tillman philosophy still seemed to govern the way black lives were valued. Fear and circumspection were necessary attributes for survival. The murder of Emmett Till in Mississippi in 1955 reminded outsiders of the lethal lawlessness of the keepers of the Southern color code.

And then came the Freedom Riders: for the most part, young adults, and blacks and whites together attempting to breathe life into the Supreme Court ruling requiring interstate travel be desegregated. Their original protest involved riding vulnerable buses through some of the toughest territory in America at that time: Birmingham and rural Alabama, on to Jackson, and then to Louisiana. As some Northern witnesses asked themselves whether these people had lost their minds, the Freedom Riders were waylaid at Anniston and their bus set on fire with them still inside (they escaped by a miracle). They were beaten in Birmingham. They kept on: through the dreaded landscape of rural Mississippi where mass arrests and the horrifying specter of Parchman, the Mississippi State Penitentiary, awaited them. Some of them were beaten bloody or had bones broken and skulls cracked.

And when some were felled and others stymied, a new wave came to forge on, and then there came another wave, and another. Older people burrowing through the routine of their lives looked up, took admiring notice, and then asked one another: "How in the world can they be that brave?" The nation was deeply moved, and the Kennedy Administration was forced to protect the Riders and push hard for a resolution of the problem.

The courage and tenacity of the Riders electrified large segments of the American public and drew them into the mid-century civil rights movement as no activity had done before. People began asking themselves: "What can I do?" Contributions flowed more freely into the coffers of the civil rights organizations. Blacks and their allies outside the South were motivated to take bolder actions themselves ("If those kids are willing to lay all that on the line, I should be able to screw up at least a little courage in order to support the movement"). Even many federal employees—some of them political appointees—joined a march against their own Justice Department in early 1963, which infuriated U. S. Attorney General Robert Kennedy.

The call for a March on Washington that summer received a rich and excited response from coast to coast. The civil rights movement of the 1960s had reached its maturity and helped produce a Civil Rights Act in 1964, a Voting Rights Act in 1965, and a "War on Poverty" the same year.

America was changed for the better by a grassroots democratic movement sparked by a few hundred (mostly) young people who were not crazy—just brave and idealistic, with wills of their own and a passion for a fairer and more democratic America.

They are true American heroes.

ILLINOIS CENTRAL TRAIN STATION

Along with Montgomery and Nashville, New Orleans was the third of the three primary staging cities. Most of the Riders who came through New Orleans traveled to Jackson by train. A new Amtrak/Greyhound station sits directly behind this building, which has been preserved but currently sits empty. Photographed April 7, 2007.

FOREWORD

DIANE MCWHORTER

The narrative of the civil rights movement has an inevitability bestowed by hindsight. It begins with the Supreme Court's 1954 *Brown* decision outlawing separate-but-equal education, moves through the stations of Alabama (Montgomery,

Birmingham, Selma), veers harrowingly into Mississippi, and winds down to the Memphis garbagemen's strike of 1968 that cost Martin Luther King, Jr., his life. In their unfolding, these future landmarks often felt random, futile if not doomed, or contingent upon the egos of the actors rather than any grand design of fate. Coming at what proved to be the midpoint of the chronicle, in 1961, the Freedom Rides initially appeared to be both a rerun and an oddity. But in breaking old ground, it ended up producing one of those unforeseen tectonic shifts at which history blithely excels.

Here are the before-and-afters. On May 3, 1961, thirteen men and women of differing races, creeds, generations, and fortunes meet at a Chinese restaurant in Washington, DC, for what some are feeling unlucky enough to call "The Last Supper." The next day they board buses, black and white together, for a tour of the still segregated South. Ten days later in Alabama comes the crucifixion. One bus of Freedom Riders is set on fire; the second drives into a savage ambush of Ku Klux Klansmen. The protest comes back to life in Mississippi, religious metaphor converting into true religion, with a mass following. By the end of the summer, the functional dynamics of the civil rights movement have altered. John F. Kennedy has been blindsided by the domestic cause that

will define his presidency. On the international front, the moral equation of the Cold War has been confounded by the starkly exposed lie beneath the promise of the Free World. Dialectically, democracy advances.

THE TERM "FREEDOM RIDES" EVENTUALLY encompassed a campaign that lasted more than seven months, involved over four hundred direct participants, and desegregated dozens of bus depots (plus some train stations and airports) from Virginia to Texas. They galvanized every branch of the civil rights movement, binding its past to its future, its tactics to its soul. But when those original thirteen Freedom Riders hit the road on May 4, 1961, they hardly seemed bound for destiny. Their sponsor, the Congress of Racial Equality, (CORE) was an artifact, a rejuvenated twenty-year-old sect of pacifist lefties, who practiced Mohandas K. Gandhi's credo of personal ethics yoked to political revolution. In 1947, using a Gandhian model of nonviolent direct action, CORE undertook its signal protest, an integrated bus ride of sixteen blacks and whites through the Upper South to test a 1946 Supreme Court decision outlawing segregated seating on interstate buses and trains. CORE's Journey of Reconciliation drew neither violent white retribution nor black enthusiasm. (Thurgood Marshall, the NAACP's top lawyer, warned his colleagues to ignore these "well-meaning radical groups.")

IT WOULD BE MORE THAN EIGHT YEARS BEFORE buses came into their own as a (literal) vehicle for civil rights, thanks to Rosa Parks, in Montgomery. The year-long bus boycott she launched there pivoted the civil rights struggle out of the courtroom, where the NAACP had pressed a Sisyphean strategy of "legalism and gradualism," and into the community, whose bus-shunning "walkers" composed a mass moral witness for justice. The boycott also made a household name of the young minister in charge, Martin Luther King, Jr.

Three years later, in 1960, King was still casting about for a post–bus boycott platform when the movement was thrust into a new phase of direct action that made prophets of CORE. In February, after four black college students took up positions at the white-only Woolworth's lunch counter in Greensboro, NC, "sit-ins" spread rapidly around the South. CORE, which had held pioneering restaurant sit-ins in Chicago not long after its founding in 1942, stepped in as a sort of board of advisers to the student activists feeling their way. Until then largely white, elite, and northern, CORE realized that the moment had come to put a charismatic African-American at its helm.

He was forty-one-year-old James Farmer, a Ph.D. with a Gandhian soul in a bon vivant's body, who had helped found CORE in the forties but had soon left, uncomfortable with its pacifist orthodoxies. Overdue to make his mark—the ascent of the younger Martin Luther King had awakened in him the "green-eyed monster" of envy—Farmer decided to inaugurate his stewardship of CORE with a calculated act of provocation.

Farmer recognized what had essentially been true since the Civil War: The South would not voluntarily grant civil rights to its second-class, black citizens. Change had to be forced on the region by the United States government. The 1960 sit-ins, because the segregation laws they challenged were local ordinances, had provided no clear pretext for a federal response. But a Supreme Court ruling that same year gave Farmer an opening. Expanding upon the 1946 decision that inspired CORE's Journey of Reconciliation, the new one decreed that segregation was illegal not just on interstate buses and trains but in the stations that served them. Accordingly, Farmer's new Freedom Riders would travel on regular Greyhound and Trailways buses into Southern depots and integrate their restaurants, restrooms, and waiting rooms. In contrast to the student sit-ins, which were law-breaking acts of civil disobedience, what the Freedom Riders were doing was perfectly legal. Nonetheless, Farmer's avowed aim was to inflame "the racists of the South to create a crisis so that the federal government would be compelled to enforce the law." In other words, he was doing exactly what the white South always accused civil rights "agitators" of: "looking for trouble."

FOILING THE FREEDOM RIDERS' REHEARSALS for violence (complete with non-simulated rib-stomping), the reception in the Upper South was benign—"They heard we were coming and baked us a cake," said one. Only three reporters, all black, were covering the event, which posed no competition for the week's major news story: America's first man in space, the Mercury astronaut Alan Shepard. When the Riders reached Atlanta on May 13 to receive Martin Luther King's good wishes, one of King's associates assured them that the white mood would be different across the state line in Alabama. In the early morning hours, Farmer's terminally ill father, a retired Howard University professor (said to have been the first black Ph.D. from Texas), died in a Washington hospital. The widow found some consolation in the fact that "Junior's" required presence at the funeral was sparing him from Birmingham, AL.

The city known as the Johannesburg of America, considered the most segregated in the country, would, not for the last time, be a make-or-break test of the civil rights movement. Looking back at the Birmingham of 1961 affords a perspective on the civil rights story that often gets lost in the telling, as a battle of good versus evil rather than good versus normal. Birmingham was a particularly vivid specimen of apartheid as it operated in the American South, one hundred years after the country had fought a civil war to redeem its birthright of equality. To visiting journalists who had covered totalitarian societies overseas, the city invited comparison to Stalinist Russia (Harrison Salisbury of the *New York Times*) and Nazi Germany (CBS's Edward R. Murrow). In response to the impending arrival of the Freedom Riders, Birmingham's top elected official, Commissioner Eugene "Bull" Connor, had ordered his police department to let the Ku Klux Klan have fifteen uninhibited minutes to give them a meaningful welcome. A Klan official claimed to have been personally instructed by Connor: "By God, if you are going to do this thing, do it right."

The Freedom Riders left Atlanta on Sunday morning, May 14, in two buses that carried regular passengers as well. The first one didn't even make it to Birmingham. A convoy of fifty cars overtook the Greyhound bus outside Anniston, and two hundred men armed with chains, clubs, and pipes charged it, with yells of "Sieg, heil!" Someone shouted, "Let's roast 'em," and a firebomb was heaved through a rear window. The Freedom Riders were taken to a local hospital, where they were largely ignored until the administration told them to leave. Their bus smoldered down to its charred steel frame, providing the first iconic image of the Freedom Ride.

The second bus rolled into Birmingham's Trailways station at 4:15 that Sunday afternoon. The captain of this leg, one of two Harvard alums on the Ride, was James Peck, the forty-six-year-old scion of the Peck & Peck New York retail family. He had been on CORE's 1947 Journey of Reconciliation and had ended up being surprised at how many drivers and passengers were tolerant of integration. Fourteen years later, he faced a crowd of white men in sports shirts, holding paper bags barely concealing lead pipes. "Before you get my brothers," he addressed them, "you will have to kill me." Five men dragged him into the alley and whaled away at him, one wielding the default weapon of southern vigilantes, the Coke bottle. Within seconds Peck went unconscious, and would require fifty-three stitches to close up his exposed skull. Inside the station, the Klansmen whipped, kicked, pummeled, and bludgeoned the Freedom Riders along with anyone else who got in their way, including the first photographer to appear on the scene. The only national reporter, CBS's Howard K. Smith, deemed it his toughest assignment since the liberation of the concentration camps.

Bull Connor was ready with a smug excuse for the absence of police officers: He had given most of his men that Sunday off because it was Mother's Day. The Klan–city hall alliance had nearly pulled off a flawless intervention, except that the smashed camera of the photographer stomped by the mob had been retrieved by a colleague. A picture on the film inside—the only known photograph of the assault—showed two white men, one cocking a lead pipe, the other baring his teeth in an expression of animal bloodlust, whipping up on an obscured victim. Printed in newspapers around the world, it commuted the shame of Birmingham into the disgrace of America. The worst of the Mother's Day scandal would not be revealed for years: The brawny man in the foreground holding down the victim was Gary Thomas Rowe, Jr., the FBI's best informant inside the Klan. When confronted with photographic evidence of its own employee's violent participation, the local FBI office covered up Rowe's crime, shielding his coconspirators in the Faustian bargain.

President Kennedy faced the second catastrophe of his new administration, barely a month after the egregious invasion of Cuba's Bay of Pigs. Focused on the impending summit in Vienna with the Soviet premier Nikita Khrushchev, Kennedy proposed a rather brusque remedy for the crisis: "Tell them to call it off. Stop them." Given that the government could not dictate the travel plans of its citizens, Robert F. Kennedy, attorney general of the United States (and the president's brother), got on the phone with a bus station manager in Birmingham and ordered him to call "Mr. Greyhound" in order to find a driver willing "to get in the damn bus and get it going and get these people on their way." (The bus drivers' union had declined a role in this civil rights drama; as one of the drivers refusing to transport the Riders put it, "I don't have but one life to give and I don't intend to give it to CORE or the NAACP, and that's all I have to say.") The prospect of spending the night in another Birmingham bus depot sapped the last of the CORE casualties' stamina. They decided to get out of town that night, on a plane.

The civil rights movement faced what was potentially a crisis of survival. Ending the Freedom Ride would ratify mob violence as a foolproof strategy of white resistance. The Rider who felt this most keenly was John Lewis, a twenty-one-year-old former "boy preacher" from Alabama, now a seminary student in Nashville. Lewis was a leader of the Nashville student movement, the most militantly effective chapter of the Student Nonviolent Coordinating Committee, known as SNCC ("Snick"), a youth organization that had formed out of the lunch-counter sit-ins of 1960. Lewis, who was on the original ride out of DC, had been forced, like Farmer, to miss the Alabama leg of the Freedom Ride, because of an interview in Philadelphia for a fellowship. Now he was back in Nashville caucusing with his fellow activists.

Among them was the equally determined Diane Nash, a Fisk University student from Chicago, so disarmingly lovely that the previous year she had elicited a confession from Nashville's mayor that segregation was morally wrong. After a night of soul-searching, some of the Nashville students wrote out their wills. Nash called Martin Luther King's lieutenant in Birmingham, Fred Shuttlesworth, to say, "Violence can't stop the rides or we are lost. I'm ready to send the students down." On Wednesday, John Lewis arrived in Birmingham with nine other students, ready to put their lives on the line for the privilege of riding a bus out of an American city.

For a couple of days, Commissioner Bull Connor toyed with the young people, first taking them into "protective custody," then personally removing them from jail, driving them to the Tennessee state line, and depositing them in the middle of pre-dawn nowhere. Diane Nash (who remained in Nashville coordinating the campaign) had reinforcements back in Birmingham that same Friday afternoon. The Freedom Bus left Birmingham on Saturday, May 20, nearly a week after Mother's Day. Its next stop was the state capital of Montgomery, where Governor John Patterson, another elected friend of the Klan, had told a reporter, irresistibly, "When these agitators go somewhere seeking trouble, they usually find it."

Sixteen state police cars and a highway patrol airplane escorted the Greyhound SceniCruiser down Highway 31, peeling off at the city limits of Montgomery. Despite the local officials' assurances to the FBI, there were no policemen at the Montgomery depot—only the usual whites bearing pipes, baseball bats, and Coke bottles, plus pocketbooks: This mob included women. Around 200 strong, they first attacked an NBC cameraman, then turned on the Riders with shouts of "Filthy Communists, nigger lovers." John Seigenthaler, the Southern-born aide whom Robert Kennedy had dispatched to the emergency in Alabama, drove his rental car into the riot. Hopping out to rescue a besieged white female Rider, he was walloped on the ear with a pipe and left on the ground unconscious. John Lewis had been brained by a wooden soft drink crate, and as he lay bleeding on the street, the attorney general of Alabama drove up and personally served him with an injunction barring future integrated rides.

The two crucial axes were now mobilized. On Sunday, May 21, both Martin Luther King and the protective apparatus of the U. S. government arrived in Montgomery. At least three senior lawyers from the Justice Department, including the future Supreme Court Justice Byron White, set up paramilitary operations at a local air force base, while King prepared for that evening's mass meeting at the church of his closest colleague,

Ralph Abernathy. The white resistance reconstituted outside. With James Farmer back from his father's funeral and SNCC's Diane Nash down from Tennessee, the high command of the civil rights movement risked being wiped out in a single blow by homicidally racist Alabamians whom Governor Patterson had recently characterized as "interested citizens."

The Justice Department "riot squad," as Kennedy's civil rights troubleshooters would henceforth be known, had rustled up a contingent of federal marshals to protect the 1,500 people who, by nightfall, were trapped inside the First Baptist. Army troops were on standby across the border in Georgia, though the president hoped to avoid invading his own country. The marshals' tear gas proved unequal to the rioters, who had set a car on fire and were hurling stink bombs through the window of the church. Only after Robert Kennedy informed the governor that troops would be flown in did Patterson consent to call out the National Guard. At 4:30 in the morning, black citizens finally received safe transport through the streets of Alabama, in the military Jeeps of the state.

ASSUMING THAT THE COLD WAR DOCTRINE of containment could be imposed on the tension between freedom and repression at home, the Kennedys had counted on resolving the Freedom Ride crisis in time to avoid "embarrassing" the president at the upcoming Vienna summit. ("Man, we've been embarrassed all our lives," Ralph Abernathy retorted.) The administration was not pleased on Wednesday when two buses left Montgomery for Jackson, Mississippi, carrying more reporters than Freedom Riders. Another busload arrived in Montgomery that afternoon from the Ivy League, led by Yale University's chaplain, William Sloane Coffin, Jr. After receiving an earful from the attorney general over the telephone, King incredulously informed his colleagues that the Kennedys didn't understand there was a "social revolution going on in the world."

The administration, however, had inexorably become part of it. On May 29, fulfilling James Farmer's original goal of federal intercession, Robert Kennedy petitioned the Interstate Commerce Commission (ICC) to draw up national regulations guaranteeing "the unquestioned right of all persons to travel through the various states without being subjected to discrimination." Meanwhile, to make sure there were no more embarrassing photographs, the Kennedys had

CORE

The Freedom Rides were originally sponsored by the Congress on Racial Equality, who sent thirteen Riders south on buses from Washington, DC, on May 4, 1961. After horrific violence in Alabama on May 14, Mother's Day, threatened to derail the Rides, members of the Nashville Student Movement stepped in to continue the Rides into Mississippi. A week after the first Riders arrived in Jackson, representatives from CORE, the Student Nonviolent Coordinating Committee (SNCC), the Southern Christian Leadership Council (SCLC), and others created an ad hoc committee to manage the Rides going forward.

worked out a plan with their realpolitik friend in the Senate, Mississippi's arch-segregationist James Eastland, to have the Riders ("Communist-inspired," Eastland charged) locked up as soon as they got off the bus in Jackson. That city now became the Freedom Riders' ultimate destination and the movement's crucial proving ground. (This under-examined chapter of the Freedom Rides is admirably chronicled in Raymond Arsenault's *Freedom Riders*, the first comprehensive account of the protest.)

Jackson was the capital of the state that fellow constituents of the Old Confederacy always "thanked God for," because it was stereotypically more wretched than theirs. For blacks, Mississippi was, as one SNCC leader put it, "the middle of the iceberg." Earlier that spring, the Jackson police department had handled demonstrations at the public library with German shepherd police dogs Rebel and Happy, whose Missouri-based trainer was, as a local daily reported without elaboration, a "former Nazi storm trooper who trained killer Dobermans to guard Hitler's airports."

The Freedom Riders on the first two buses into Mississippi were accompanied by National Guardsmen in the aisles bearing rifles with bayonets fixed—making their businesslike reception in Jackson seem almost surreal. Debarking from the bus, they found themselves flanked by policemen on their left and right, giving them no choice but to go straight to the white waiting room. Police captain J. L. Ray confronted the Riders with an impassive, "Move on." When they refused, they were escorted right to the waiting police wagons. "We didn't realize it at the time," Dave Dennis, a twenty-year-old student from New Orleans who was on the first bus, recalled, "but we were really under arrest from the time we left Montgomery until the time we got to Jackson."

In a maneuver typical of the South's defenders, the state avoided booking them under racially discriminatory statutes, lest it give the movement a legal pretext to mount a Constitutional challenge to segregation. On the grounds that public safety was at stake, the Riders were charged with "breach of the peace."

"I feel wonderful," Mississippi's governor Ross Barnett said of the slick operation in Jackson. "I'm so happy everything went off so smoothly." In contrast to the crude showboating of Birmingham's Bull Connor, Jackson's mayor Allen Thompson played the event as a press opportunity, presenting out-of-town reporters with honorary police badges and then packing them off on a bus tour of the city.

The Kennedy-Eastland deal prevented mob violence, but it also ensured that Jackson would remain the focal point of the protest. Under arrest and unable to continue on to New Orleans, the destination of James Farmer's original Freedom Ride, the activists decided to pursue a "jail, no bail" strategy. This Gandhian precept combined two essential pieces of the liberation process: personal sacrifice, a willingness to pay the price for one's principles, and non-cooperation (in the sense of refusing any cash commerce) with the evil institutions under protest. A further aim was to discombobulate the system by filling the jails.

By mid-June, Jackson's city and county jails were so crowded with Freedom Riders from around the country that the authorities decided to transfer them 120 miles away to Parchman, the most notorious prison in the South. All the Riders were put in maximum security, including the white women, whom Southern white psyches placed in a (sexual) category of "nigger lover," even more despicable than that of the white men. Isolated on an 18,000-acre prison farm deep in the Delta and denied the modest dignities of bodily cleanliness, fresh air, and motion, the Freedom Riders were forced back on their deepest resources as individuals; their means of solidarity were no more palpable than the freedom songs they sang to keep up their morale and, in what was becoming a deliberate strategy of the movement, drive their white minders crazy. "They turned off the air conditioner and the water because we wouldn't stop singing," Rip Patton, a student from Tennessee State University, recalled of the Fourth of July he spent in Parchman. "So, it was hot and a little smelly because we couldn't flush the toilets . . . But we kept singing. That singing, they just couldn't handle it."

As of mid-September, nearly three hundred Freedom Riders (some traveling by train and even a few by plane) had been locked up in Mississippi. The volunteers joining the core of black and white students were an astoundingly ecumenical group: a painter, a New York assemblyman, a social worker, a professional boxer, a homemaker, and New York governor Nelson Rockefeller's son-in-law. That is not to say that the Freedom Rides had broad support. The consensus of public opinion all summer long seemed to be that the Riders had made their point in Alabama: the continuing effort in Mississippi was, as the *New York Times* put it, "overreaching." The *Times* editors found themselves eating their words on September 21, grudgingly acknowledging that the Freedom Rides had gotten results: In response to the Kennedys' petition, the ICC issued an unexpectedly unanimous and strongly worded ruling banning segregation in all facilities serving interstate passengers.

The stalemate between the Freedom Riders and the state of Mississippi dragged on, since the ICC ruling was not to go into effect until November. The Mississippi officials had forced the movement to play on terms that historically proved advantageous to white people—money—with onerous fines and expensive appellate protocols intended to drain the Freedom Rides' operating fund. Perhaps the ultimate achievement of the Freedom Riders was that, even as the headlines faded in the summer, and without knowing what the results would be, they kept coming, simply because what they were doing had to be done. The resulting moral clarity, combined with the prodigious organizational and fundraising skills honed in its service, completed the Freedom Rides' evolution from what had arguably been a courageous stunt by James Farmer to the kind of transformative community-building discipline that would sustain the movement into its future.

The nation moved on to other crises. In August, on the heels of President Kennedy's shaky summit with Khrushchev, the Communists had erected an "anti-fascist protection wall" in the contested Cold War trophy of Berlin, bringing the world powers closer to hot, thermonuclear conflict. Segregation would not be abolished for nearly three years, by the Civil Rights Act of 1964. It was the great, posthumous achievement of John F. Kennedy, who had introduced the bill after Bull Connor sicced police dogs on child demonstrators during Martin Luther King's turning-point campaign of 1963 in Birmingham. The Selma to Montgomery March two years later, leading to the equally monumental Voting Rights Act of 1965, would be the grand finale of the powerful movement coalition forged in the Freedom Rides. The next year, over John Lewis' anguished objections, a disillusioned SNCC largely abandoned King's nonviolent dream of integration in favor of the militant separatism of Black Power, whose avatar, Stokely Carmichael, had undergone his movement baptism as a Freedom Rider in Parchman prison. By the end of his life, King had himself come to despair of overcoming the "triplets of social misery": racism, poverty, and war, specifically in Vietnam.

John Lewis is now one of the most respected members of the U.S. House of Representatives. So it goes with the American meta-story, that eternal tug-of-war between power and justice, sin and glory. The Freedom Rides were a microcosm of that process, the worst in our national character inspiring the best. Sometimes, the abstractions of history make us lose sight of what the men and women on the following pages so movingly demonstrate. The lofty course of human events is only a series of individual lives, in all their particularity and universality, their mortality and grandeur: the blind faith of the actors (and this was equally true of the antagonists) that they will come out on the right side of history. No one can predict which ones among us will be "tracked down by the Zeitgeist," as Martin Luther King said of Rosa Parks. But as these witnesses prove, there is no duty as basic, yet so potentially heroic, as getting on the bus.

GATE ONE (MAIN ENTRANCE), PARCHMAN

Three weeks after the first buses arrived in Jackson, Freedom Riders had
succeeded in their goal of filling the city's jails. Officials began transferring
them to Parchman, the state prison, 130 miles north in the Delta. Every
Rider who did not bail out early did time there, most in maximum-security.
For a few weeks at the height of the Rides, the white men were housed in a
new barracks-styled building known as the first offenders' camp.
Photographed July 28, 2006.

INTRODUCTION

ERIC ETHERIDGE

I lived just sixty miles north of Jackson, in a little town called Carthage, at the time of the Freedom Rides. I was four and not yet aware of my state's troubled racial history or the emerging civil rights movement.

I lived with my parents in a house a short car-ride from the town square. That's where I hung out as I got older, mostly at the drug store with the soda fountain, the movie theater, and another drug store where no one ever said anything if I sat on the windowsill and read war comic books without buying them. My grandfather had once owned a hardware store on the square. Now he and a partner were in the chicken business, and my father worked for them. I would occasionally go see him at the company's processing plant, which slaughtered and dressed hundreds of chickens a day. The plant sat back-to-back with the Carthage Bank, which anchored the southeast corner of the square.

The issue of race was present everywhere—in my school (separate but equal), in my doctor's office (separate entrances and waiting rooms), at my church (whites only), and at the movie theater (blacks had to sit in the balcony). But I remained for the most part unaware of the various campaigns of direct action and voter registration that the state's black citizens, organized by the NAACP and SNCC, CORE and COFO, were waging in Jackson, McComb, Greenwood, and many other towns.

Those campaigns were history by the time I came of age in the seventies and headed north, first to college in Nashville, then again in 1979 to New York City in hopes of becoming a magazine editor. Though the stops were mostly all good,

after sixteen years in magazines and another eight online, creating and running websites, I was growing restless, tired of trying to realize other people's projects. For several years I had been taking pictures with increasing ambition. Looking for a project to assign myself, I turned my attention south, toward home, where I knew the files of the State Sovereignty Commission, Mississippi's "segregation watchdog" in the fifties and sixties, had recently been made public. I wondered if they contained any photographs I could work with.

After a few calls I was on the phone with the friend of a friend who worked at the state's Department of Archives and History, which now had possession of the files. Yes, she told me, there were a number of photographs, about 500 or so. But most of them, she said, were just mug shots.

MISSISSIPPI ESTABLISHED THE STATE Sovereignty Commission in 1956, two years after *Brown* vs. *Board of Education,* and empowered it "to do and perform any and all acts and things deemed necessary and proper to protect the sovereignty of the State of Mississippi, and her sister states, from the encroachment thereon by the Federal Government."

As it turned out, any and all things necessary included hiring a former FBI agent as one of its investigators and establishing a network of informants throughout the state to report on the doings of anyone who showed the slightest inclination to think or act differently on matters of race. It also included funneling public funds, as much as $5,000 a month, to the White Citizens' Council, a private organization that some saw as the more pious and energetic defender of the Southern way of life. The Citizens' Council had itself been created in the Mississippi Delta town of Indianola a scant two months after Black Monday, as the day of the *Brown* decision was known. By 1961 it had a thriving membership throughout the south.

Zack J. Van Landingham was the former FBI agent. According to Yasuhiro Katagiri's history of the agency, *The Mississippi State Sovereignty Commission*, he had once served as an aide to J. Edgar Hoover. Van Landingham's first major contribution was to bring bureau rigor to the commission's filing system. In a memo dated June 5, 1959, he instituted a new process for handling the office mail and established a new index-card system for tracking the commission's many investigations. "Make a minimum of two copies of all memos, reports, letters," he wrote. "If logical and need more, make necessary number, depending on outgoing number." Along with instructions for what text to put where on the index cards—the first line should read "Last name, First, Middle"—Van Landingham also laid down the thirteen primary "case classifications." At number one was "Race Agitators," at number thirteen "Subversion."

Two years later, when the Freedom Riders began arriving, all the paperwork the commission generated in response was given a classification of two, which denoted "Integration Organizations." The specific arrangement with the Jackson police is not documented anywhere in the files, but commission investigators were routinely sent to get copies of whatever information the police had on the Riders—primarily the basic arrest data: name, height, hair and eye color, race and sex, birthday, birth city, current address—along with the mug shot.

Investigators Virgil Downing and Andy Hopkins combined to handle the first two groups of Riders, reporting their results in a May 31 memo (reproduced on pages 30-31). "We were ordered by Albert Jones, Director of the State Sovereignty Commission to make a complete coverage of the arrival of two groups of integrationist, so-called Freedom Riders, that arrived on two separate buses from Montgomery, Alabama, on

May 24, 1961. . . . A copy of all names and pictures of each individual including criminal records of each individual of the first group of so-called Freedom Riders is attached to this report."

A couple of paragraphs down, Downing and Hopkins report the same for the second group of "so-called Freedom Riders." They add that all the Riders have been convicted of breach of the peace and turned over to the sheriff to serve their terms.

Over the next few months, as Riders continued to arrive, the memos shortened considerably. Terse and to the point, the investigators no longer even mustered the effort to insert "so-called" in front of "Freedom Riders."

BY THE TIME THE LAST FREEDOM RIDERS were arrested—fifteen Episcopal priests on September 13th at the Trailways station—Downing and Hopkins had collected mug shots and arrest data on 310 people, plus an additional eighteen men and women—all black, almost all from Mississippi—who had been arrested in related demonstrations in a city park, at a lunch counter, and at a hotel (during a meeting of the southern governors). The eighteen were convicted of breach of peace, just as those arrested at the bus and train stations, and their mug shots collected and filed by the Sovereignty Commission. Thus their inclusion here.

Most of the Mississippi Riders were young: forty percent were between the ages of eighteen and twenty-one; seventy-five percent were between eighteen and thirty. They came from all over: from thirty-nine states and ten other countries, counting by birthplace. Counting by current address (as of 1961), the distribution is somewhat more concentrated, showing the results of family migrations and collegiate choices. Fifty-four Riders came from New York state; seventy-eight— nearly one in four—came from California. These, along with others, would comprise the well-known "outside agitators" heading to Jackson.

Ninety-five Riders—almost one in three— were inside agitators, coming from Mississippi, Louisiana, Tennessee, Alabama, and Georgia. All but two of those ninety-five were black.

Overall, half of the Riders were black, half white. Women accounted for a quarter of the Riders.

THE SUNSHINE-BRIGHT IRONY IN ALL THIS, of course, is just how well the Sovereignty Commission documented what was happening in

Mississippi. When the agency was finally abolished, in 1977 (it had been all but officially dead since 1973), there was a brief struggle over its files. Burn them, said one state representative. Instead, the commission's six filing cabinets were sealed, locked, and delivered to an underground vault, the state's Vital Records Center. Twenty-one years and much legal wrangling later (extremely short version: the Mississippi ACLU sued the state and won), the files were turned over to the state's Department of Archives and History and opened to the public, available on microfilm in MDAH reading rooms. Four years later, in 2002, the archivists at the MDAH published every page from the files online.

That's where I first saw the mug shots, in early 2004. Even as low-resolution scans, the images had a compelling immediacy and intensity.

In terms of format they're standard issue—two poses on a 4" x 5" sheet. Each Rider faces the camera and stands in profile, an identity board hung by a chain around the neck. In some of the mug shots, the camera or the subject or both are positioned to reveal a metal disc atop a metal pole behind the Rider, perhaps a posing aide or camera target. (When the disc shows behind a rider's head, it sometimes looks like a miniature halo from a Renaissance painting.)

Once made, the mug shots were treated like documents, which is to say stapled, hole-punched and filed. And as documents they are powerful symbols of the repressive surveillance state. But in the same way the Freedom Riders were using the power of the state's criminal system against itself, they were also hijacking the booking process, enabling the state to record its own strategic blunder, its own tragic actions. With assistance from the Sovereignty Commission's inadvertent archivists, the mug shots now comprise a rich historical record.

Here is a picture of the emergent civil rights movement plunging forward, adeptly taking its strategy of nonviolent direct action to the national stage. Here are the faces of the student-powered sixties, working west from Greensboro and Nashville through Jackson, soon to hit Berkeley, where the Free Speech movement would ignite in 1964 with the on-campus arrest of a CORE hawker. Here is history told at the individual level: 328 black and white men and women who felt compelled to put themselves in harm's way in

Mississippi, each singularly recorded and documented.

Placed before the camera, some of the Riders look down or away; others meet its gaze with their own. As portraits, the mug shots are always compelling and frequently stellar. The police camera caught something special, even if no one quite intended it that way. I was captivated by these images and wanted to bring them to a wider audience. I wanted to find the Riders today, to look into their faces, to make new portraits to set against the earlier photographs.

THE FIRST CALLS TO FORMER RIDERS WERE invariably a surprise to them. Many were immediately ready to talk, to share their story, to make plans to get together. Others took a few minutes, or longer, to sort through my story before opening up. Over time I found the quickest way to an easy conversation was to say, early on, "I have your mug shot from 1961. Have you ever seen it?" Several had but most had not, and the idea that it still existed seemed to captivate them.

I started meeting Riders and making portraits in 2005. Most of the portraits were taken on several long trips which began in the fall of 2006 and ended the next summer. I usually met the Riders in their homes. Our sessions lasted on average three hours, the first of which was spent doing an interview. Then we made a picture.

So far I have photographed just over a hundred Riders. A few I have contacted I have yet to visit and photograph, due to distant locations or schedules that didn't work the first time around. A handful of Riders refused to be photographed. Approximately eighty are dead. All of which leaves roughly 140 I haven't been able to find. My hope is that the publication of this book will mean many more additions to the series.

ONCE COLLECTED AND FILED, WERE THE MUG shots ever looked at again? I didn't find any evidence of that, even though many of the Riders continued to work in the movement in Mississippi. If the portraits proved of little use to the Sovereignty Commission, they're invaluable to us today. They give us the chance to take the measure of these men and women in the very heat of battle, and perhaps to take measure of ourselves in their responding gáze. Here they are, four decades later, patiently and urgently awaiting our reply.

TITLE: Freedon Riders
* *

INVESTIGATIVE PERIOD: May 24, through May 30, 1961
* * * * ** ** * * * * * * * * * * * * * * * * * * * * * * * * * *

DATE OF REPORT: May 31, 1961
* *

INVESTIGATED BY: Virgil Downing and Andy Hopkins, Investigators
* * * * ** *

APPROVED BY: _____
* *

TYPED BY: Marie Rayfield
* *

     We were ordered by Albert Jones, Director of the State Sover-
eignty Commission to make a complete coverage of the arrival of two
groups of integrationist, so-called Freedom Riders, that arrived on
two separate buses from Montgomery, Alabama on May 24, 1961 on the
Continential Trailway Bus line company. The Continential Trailway
Bus terminal is located in Jackson, Mississippi at 201 East Pascagoula
Street. We were ordered by Director Jones, of the State Sovereignty
Commission to obtain all names of each individual freedom rider and
to get all information of each individual that participated in the
violation of the constituted laws of the State of Mississippi.

     We arrived at the Continential Trailway Bus terminal located
at 201 East Pascagoula Street, Jackson, Mississippi about 1:30 p.m.,
May 24, 1961. The first group of so-called Freedom Riders arrived
at the bus terminal at about 1:55 p.m., May 24, 1961 and after they
refused to obey the orders of the Jackson Police Officers by refusing to move on, they were arrested for violating section 2087.5
and they were placed under arrest by police officers of the Jackson
Police Department and was remanded to the Jackson City Jail for trial.
Acopy of all names and pictures of each individual,including criminal
records of each individual of the first group of the so-called Freedom
Riders is attached to this report which consist of twelve persons.

     The second group of so-called Freedom Riders arrived by Con-
tinential Trailway Bus Lines in Jackson, Mississippi on May 24, 1961
at the Continential Bus terminal, located at 201 East Pascagoula Street,
Jackson, Mississippi about 4:45 p.m. and after they refused to obey
the orders of the Jackson Police by refusing to move on, they were
arrested by police officers of the Jackson Police Department for violating
section 2087.5 of the constitution and was remanded to Jackson City jail

2-55-207

TITLE: Freedom Riders

for trial. A copy of all names and pictures of each individual including criminal records of each individual of the second group of
the so-called Freedom Riders is attached to this report which consists
of fifteen persons.

The trial of all twenty-seven persons of the so-called Freedom
Riders of both groups that arrived in Jackson, Mississippi from Montgomery, Alabama on May 24, 1961 by Continential Trailway Bus were
tried in the Jackson Police Court after they had declined bail on
charges that they had disobeyed an officer and the breach of the peace.
All twenty-seven of the so-called Freedom Riders were found guilty of
breach of the peace under section 2087.5 and were sentenced by the
Municipal Court Judge, James L. Spencer, to pay a fine of $200.00 and
serve 60 days in jail. The 60 day jail sentence was suspended by
Judge Spencer.

All twenty-seven persons of the so-called Freedom Riders were
turned over to the Sheriff of Hinds County, Mississippi, Sheriff
J. R. (Bob) Gilfoy) to serve out their sentence. We were informed
by Sheriff Gilfoy that five of the so-called Freedom Riders made a
$500.00 cash bond, posted by (C. O. R. E) Congress of Racial Equality.

This concludes our assignment and is the end of our report.

-2-

TRAILWAYS

MAY 24

Montgomery to Jackson

Julia Aaron
20875 New Orleans, LA - Age 20

Alexander Anderson
20872 Nashville, TN - Age 33

Harold Andrews
20882 Atlanta, GA - Age 23 - Died 1976

James Bevel
20879 Nashville, TN - Age 24

Joseph Carter
20878 Nashville, TN - Age 22 - Died 2006

Paul Deitrich
20873 Washington, DC - Age 29 - Died 2005

Dave Dennis
20883 New Orleans, LA - Age 20

Bernard LaFayette, Jr.
20877 Nashville, TN - Age 20

Rev. James Lawson
20880 Nashville, TN - Age 32

Jean Thompson
20874 New Orleans, TN - Age 19

Rev. C. T. Vivian
20881 Nashville, TN - Age 36

Matthew Walker, Jr.
20876 Nashville, TN - Age 19

DAVE DENNIS

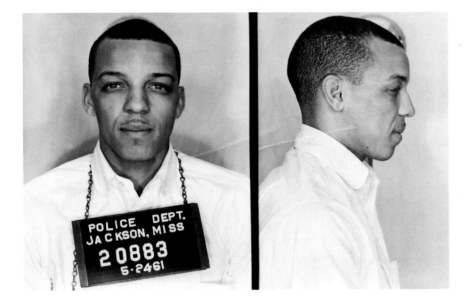

POLICE DEPT.
JACKSON, MISS
20883
5-24-61

We did not believe we would make it to Jackson. We did not know if we would get out of Montgomery. At that point, we didn't particularly trust the police or even the National Guard. We were prepared, mentally, to expect the worst. We weren't ready to give our lives, but we were not afraid to die.

BORN

October 17, 1940, on a plantation outside Omega, LA. Grew up primarily on the Miles Plantation, outside of Shreveport, LA, and in the Cedar Grove area of Shreveport.

THEN

Student at Dillard University, New Orleans; active in the civil rights movement.

SINCE THEN

Became a CORE field secretary in the fall of 1961, organizing in Shreveport and Baton Rouge, LA, then in Mississippi from 1962-65. Was co-director , with Bob Moses, of COFO and Freedom Summer in 1964. Also worked extensively on the Mississippi Freedom Democratic Party.

Returned to Dillard University in 1965 and graduated three years later. Earned a law degree from the University of Michigan, Ann Arbor, in 1971, and practiced in New Orleans and Baton Rogue. Since 1991 has worked with Bob Moses' Algebra Project, which aims to improve the teaching of math to black high school students. Currently heads the Algebra Project in New Orleans, Petersburg, VA, and South Carolina. Also works with the Vanguard Foundation to develop affordable housing in historically black neighborhoods in New Orleans.

Photographed
March 28, 2007
New Orleans, LA
Age: 66

REV. JAMES LAWSON

I did not begin to call what I was doing non-violence until 1947, when I accepted the language of [pacifist] A.J. Muste and Gandhi. That's when I started using the language of non-violence for myself. Until that time, I was using the language of love as I found that in Jesus of Nazareth, and as my parents, especially as my mother, influenced me.

Jesus provided me with the spirituality of the nonviolence. Jesus was my first source. But Gandhi was the man who showed me the methodology of nonviolence.

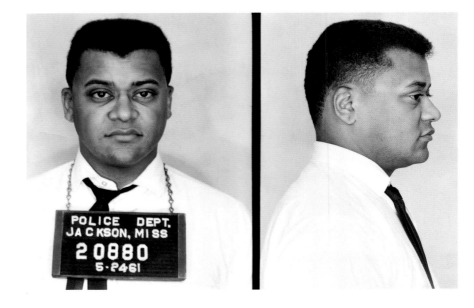

BORN

September 22, 1928, in Uniontown, PA. Grew up in Massillon, OH. Son and grandson of Methodist ministers. Joined CORE in 1948, his freshman year at Baldwin Wallace College in Berea, OH. Withdrew his draft registration in 1949, later served thirteen months in federal prison. Was a missionary to India 1953–56.

THEN

Methodist minister and divinity student in Nashville; in 1959 began a weekly nonviolence workshop, from which emerged the Nashville Student Movement and, in large part, SNCC. Expelled from Vanderbilt University Divinity School in 1960 for his activities as a leader of the Nashville sit-ins.

SINCE THEN

Pastor, Centenary Methodist Church, Memphis, 1962–74; helped organize the Meredith March in Mississippi in 1966; head of the Memphis sanitation workers' strike committee in 1968. Pastor of the Holman United Methodist Church, Los Angeles, 1974–99. Named Vanderbilt's Distinguished Alumnus of the Year in 2005; has been a visiting professor at the Divinity School since 2006.

Photographed
November 11, 2005
Los Angeles, CA
Age: 77

POLICE   DEPT.
JA C KSON, MI SS
20874
5-2461

JEAN THOMPSON

My parents always talked about the injustice of segregation, but they were optimistic; they didn't feel like it was going to last forever. They raised us to be ready. I remember my dad saying the day will come, and when the day comes, you should be ready.

My father was in Colorado, looking for work, when I was arrested in Jackson, and he found out that I was slapped [during an interrogation]. That was how he found out I was a Freedom Rider. When I got back home he called and said, "What are you doing this for?"

I had to remind him that this is what you told us to do. So, he didn't say anything.

Then I said, "And by the way, Shirley [her sister] is gonna go tomorrow [to Mississippi as a Freedom Rider]."

He said, "Let me talk to your mother."

BORN
January 13, 1942, in Lake Providence, LA. Grew up there and in New Orleans.

THEN
Active in New Orleans CORE, along with her sisters, Alice and Shirley. Shirley was arrested at the Trailways station on June 6th.

SINCE THEN
After bailing out of jail in Jackson, she returned to New Orleans to train Freedom Riders about to go into Jackson. Continued to do sit-ins and picketing for several years. She also did civil rights work elsewhere in the south, including Canton, MS, after Medgar Evers was murdered, and in North Carolina.

Moved to New York City in the mid-sixties, where she worked with local CORE chapters. In the late sixties she was involved in civil rights, anti-war, and feminist efforts in Berkeley and San Francisco.

She has lived in Amherst, MA, since the early seventies.

Photographed
June 23, 2007
Amherst, MA
Age: 65

BERNARD LAFAYETTE, JR.

BORN
July 29, 1940, in Tampa, FL. Grew up in Tampa and Philadelphia.

THEN
Student at the American Baptist Theological Seminary, in Nashville; a leader of the Nashville Student Movement. Stayed in Jackson after bailing out to recruit new Freedom Riders and organize the Jackson Nonviolent Movement.

SINCE THEN
Worked for the SCLC and helped run numerous campaigns, including Selma, AL, in 1961 and 1965, and the Alabama Voter Registration Project in 1962. Served as the national coordinator for the Poor Peoples' Campaign in 1968.

Has taught and been an administrator at several universities and colleges. Currently heads the Center for Nonviolence and Peace Studies at the University of Rhode Island.

Photographed
July 10, 2007
Kingston, RI
Age: 66

REV. C.T. VIVIAN

BORN
July 28, 1924, in Howard, MO. Grew up there and in Macomb, IL. Graduated from Western Illinois University in 1946. Participated in his first sit-in in 1947 in Peoria, successfully integrating a cafeteria.

THEN
Student at the American Baptist Theological Seminary in Nashville; a leader of the Nashville Student Movement.

SINCE THEN
Joined the executive staff of Southern Christian Leadership Conference in 1963, helping to plan and lead campaigns in Birmingham, St. Augustine, Selma, and elsewhere. Moved to Chicago in 1966 to run the Urban Training Center for Christian Mission and the Coalition for United Community Action. Later founded the Black Strategies and Information Center, the National Center for Human Rights Education, and the Center for Democratic Renewal. Lives in Atlanta.

Photographed
May 8, 2007
Atlanta, GA
Age: 82

MATTHEW WALKER, JR.

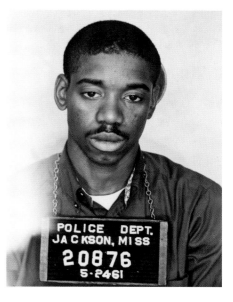

When we got to Mississippi, National Guardsmen boarded the bus with fixed bayonets on their rifles. They stood the length of the bus in the aisle. I said to one of them, "Man, that's a mighty fancy rifle you've got there."

His response was, "I ain't got one word to say to you." [*Laughs.*]

"Yeah," I said to myself, "These are our protectors."

BORN

June 1, 1941, in Nashville and grew up there. His father was a surgeon and chairman of the surgery department at Meharry Medical College, and a member of the Nasvhille Christian Leadership Council.

THEN

Sophomore at Fisk University. Very active in the Nashville Student Movement.

SINCE THEN

Returned to Fisk University for an additional year, then joined the army in 1962 and served three years. Attended Columbia University in New York City from 1965-68, and was involved in the 1968 uprising there. Dropped out and started organizing. Among his early efforts were rent strikes in Harlem.

In 1970 went to work as an organizer for the Commission for Racial Justice, an organization supported by the Church of Christ. Worked for the commission in several locations, including Philadelphia, Washington, DC, and North Carolina. From 1982-90, organized state workers in Louisiana and hospitality workers in New Orleans for the AFL-CIO. Returned to Nashville in the late nineties. Still active in local politics, focusing on environmental issues and the public schools.

Photographed
May 25, 2007
Nashville, TN
Age: 65

GREYHOUND

MAY 24

Montgomery to Jackson

Peter Ackerberg
20892 Yellow Springs, OH - Age 22

Doris Jean Castle
20887 New Orleans, LA - Age 18 - Died 1998

Lucretia Collins
20888 Nashville, TN - Age 21

Rev. John Copeland
20884 Nashville, TN - Age 44 - Died 1987

Dion Diamond
20897 Washington, DC - Age 19

Rev. Grady Donald
20898 Nashville, TN - Age 31 - Died 2002

James Farmer
20885 New York, NY - Age 41 - Died 1999

Frank Holloway
20889 Atlanta, GA - Age 22

John Lewis
20886 Nashville, TN - Age 21

John Moody
20896 Washington, DC - Age 30

Ernest "Rip" Patton, Jr.
20890 Nashville, TN - Age 21

Jerome Smith
20893 New Orleans, LA - Age 22

Clarence Thomas
20891 Nashville, TN - Age 20

Hank Thomas
20894 Washington, DC - Age 19

LeRoy Wright
20895 Nashville, TN - Age 19

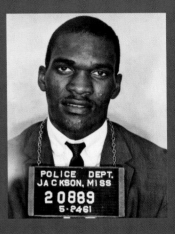

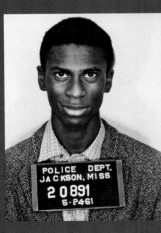

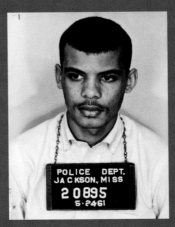

POLICE DEPT.
JACKSON, MISS
20892
5-24-61

PETER ACKERBERG

BORN
April 19, 1939, in the Bronx, NY, and grew up there.

THEN
Student, Antioch College, Yellow Springs, OH.

SINCE THEN
Graduated from Antioch in 1964 and Columbia Journalism School in 1965. Worked as a reporter at the *Minneapolis Star* from 1965 to 1982. Also got a law degree during his last years at the paper. Worked in the Minnesota state attorney general's office from 1985–1999. Now works on his own on legal projects.

Photographed
November 16, 2006
Minneapolis, MN
Age: 67

I was already in Montgomery, working for the summer for a local publisher who was an old New Dealer, when the Freedom Riders came to town and were badly beaten.

I thought to myself, "You know, I talk a big radical game, but I've never really done anything. What am I going to tell my children when they ask me about this time?"

The next day was the day the Freedom Riders were going to leave for Jackson, and I decided that I was going to go. I went down to the bus station. There was a cordon of National Guardsmen with their rifles. I told a Guardsman that I wanted to get a ticket to Jackson and he let me through. I got the ticket and got on the bus. I didn't know any of the other people on it. I sat next to Jim Farmer. I knew who he was and I sat next to him because I thought somehow, "They won't attack him."

I remember smoking away nervously, and Farmer smoking, too. The black guys and girls were singing. I was pretty scared. I sang along with the songs that I knew. They were so spirited and so unafraid. They were really prepared to risk their lives for this, and they were having a good time.

It was a highlight of my life. I'm very proud of it. But reflecting on it later, I realized that I wasn't very courageous, really, because I wasn't willing to die. I had plotted out the odds a bit. I just felt that the Kennedy Administration would not let something bad happen after the beatings in Montgomery and Anniston. These other guys, they were going ahead no matter what. Danger or not, they were committed. I was so awed by that. In my mind I was a participant, but I was also an observer.

FRANK HOLLOWAY

Nonviolence wasn't necessarily a way of life, but it was a tactic. We felt like it was a tactic that worked.

Now, the person that you'd want to hit back, yeah, yeah, yeah. Especially when you felt like somebody really took advantage of you because they knew you weren't going to hit them back. It was a challenge and it sort of made you feel good that you could do it, that you could take the abuse from them and still continue to do what you do. Because it showed white folks that these negroes are not afraid.

I mean, "I done cursed them, spit on them, hit them, beat them, and they still come back." And it also helped the people that we were working with in the community to see these young people who are not afraid. "I've been afraid of this all my life and now here are these young people — if they're not afraid, why am I?" That was the kind of thing that made you feel good about what you were doing.

I can't speak for nobody else, but I know for myself, I felt that this was what I was supposed to do. I didn't feel like I was a hero or anything like that. I just felt that this was what I was supposed to do. And I did it and when I stopped doing it, I didn't feel like anybody needed to reward me or congratulate me or pat me on my back. I did what I felt like I had to do.

BORN
February 8, 1939, in Atlanta, and grew up there.

THEN
Student and member of the Committee on Appeal for Human Rights, the organizing body of the Atlanta Student Movement; active in sit-ins and picketing, arrested several times.

SINCE THEN
Worked as a SNCC field secretary in Mississippi, Alabama, and Georgia from 1961–67.

Has spent his career working for poverty and employment agencies, including Economic Opportunity Atlanta and the Fulton Atlanta Community Action Authority, which specializes in training people and helping them find jobs.

Photographed
May 9, 2007
Atlanta, GA
Age: 68

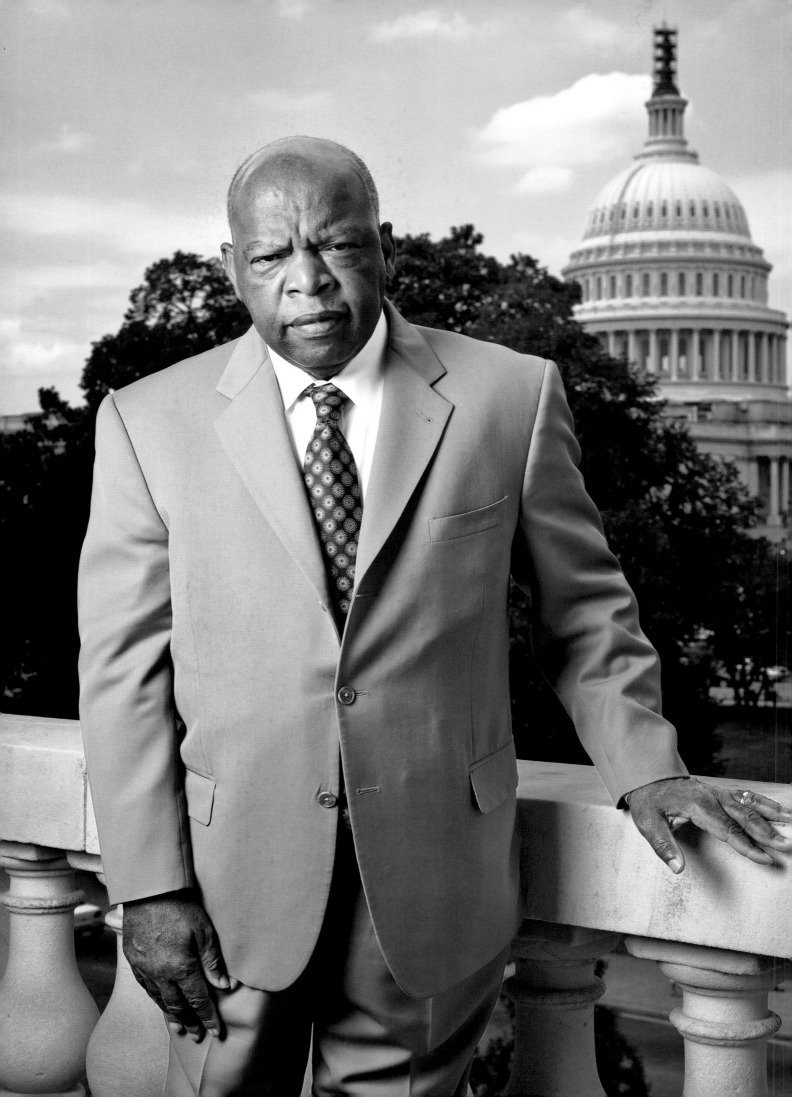

JOHN LEWIS

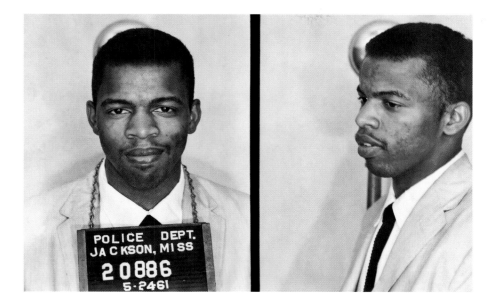

BORN

February 21, 1940, in Troy, AL, and grew up there.

THEN

Student, American Bible Theological Seminary, Nashville. A leader of the Nashville Student Movement and the sit-in campaign there in 1960. One of the original thirteen Freedom Riders who left Washington, DC, on May 4, 1961.

SINCE THEN

Head of SNCC from 1963 to 1966. A keynote speaker at the March on Washington in 1963. One of the leaders of the Selma March in 1965. Served on the Atlanta city council from 1981 to 1987. Has represented Georgia's 5th congressional district, which includes Atlanta and the surrounding area, in the House of Representatives since 1987.

Photographed
July 25, 2007
Washington, DC
Age: 67

Those of us in Nashville, that small group, we were committed to this idea of the beloved community, the redeemed America.

During our stay in Jackson and in Parchman, there was this commitment, almost a bond, that we would do everything possible to get everyone to adhere to the philosophy and discipline of nonviolence. That we would not let anything break that.

But the Freedom Rides not only took the movement off of college campuses and out of selected communities, it took it to a much larger community. The movement became much more inclusive. People saw these young Freedom Riders—and some not-so-young—getting on buses, traveling through the South, which was very dangerous. So people were willing and ready to become part of that effort.

So when people left Parchman and went to southwest Georgia and the black belt of Alabama, to Arkansas and eastern North Carolina and other parts of Mississippi, and stayed there and started working, it became a different movement.

These new people were not altogether grounded in the philosophy and discipline of nonviolence. But they wanted to be part of this effort to change America. They had a degree of freshness and a greater degree of urgency. What I call militant nonviolence, or nonviolent militancy. These young people—and those not so young—were demanding change now. And by 1963, you had people in SNCC, even someone like myself, saying "We want out Freedom, and we want it now."

HANK THOMAS

- - - - - - - - -

We'd heard about Parchman.
We'd heard about the number of blacks who went to Parchman who never returned. We also knew that Parchman was way out in the country someplace.

Some of the guards in Jackson would tell us, "Y'all get up there at Parchman, they're gonna straighten you all out. And there ain't no Robert Kennedy or John Kennedy gonna do anything about it." And people began to think that.

But me and lots of the other folks didn't buy it. When we get there, we're still going to do things our way.

But the dehumanizing process started as soon as we got there. We were told to strip naked and then walked down this long corridor. For some of us who were born and bred in the South and used to go skinny-dipping, it was no big deal. But I'll never forget Jim Farmer, a very dignified man. And here he is walking down this long corridor naked. That is dehumanizing. And that was the whole purpose.

BORN
August 29, 1941, in Jacksonville, FL. Grew up primarily in St. Augustine, FL.

THEN
Sophomore, Howard University, Washington, DC. Active in the student movement there. One of the original thirteen Freedom Riders who left Washington, DC, on May 4, 1961, and was on the bus firebombed outside Anniston, AL, on May 14.

SINCE THEN
Became a field secretary for CORE in 1962, working in Birmingham and Huntsville, AL. Inducted into the Army in 1963 and chose to serve as a medic. Did a tour of duty in Vietnam 1965–66.

Moved to Atlanta after Vietnam and got in the franchise business, starting with a laundromat, followed by a Dairy Queen. Today he and his wife own two McDonald's and four Marriott hotels; they live in Stone Mountain, GA.

Photographed
May 10, 2007
Stone Mountain, GA
Age: 65

GREYHOUND

MAY 28

Nashville to Jackson

Catherine Burks-Brooks
20909 Nashville, TN - Age 21

William Harbour
20902 Nashville, TN - Age 19

Frederick Leonard
20903 Nashville, TN - Age 18

Lester McKinnie
20901 Nashville, TN - Age 21

William Mitchell, Jr.
20904 Nashville, TN - Age 18 - Died 2003

Etta Simpson
20906 Nashville, TN - Age 19

Mary Smith
20907 Nashville, TN - Age 19

Frances Wilson
20908 Nashville, TN - Age 22

Clarence Wright
20905 Nashville, TN - Age 19 - Died 1975

CATHERINE BURKS-BROOKS

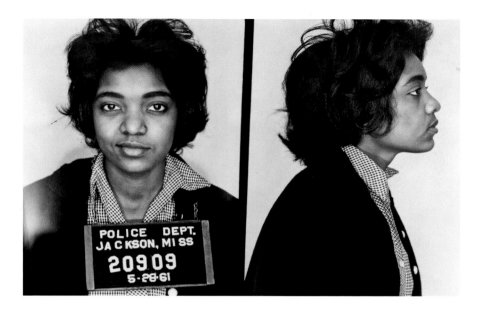

BORN

October 8, 1939, in Birmingham, AL, and grew up there.

THEN

Senior, Tennessee State, Nashville; active in the Nashville movement.

SINCE THEN

Worked in Mississippi on voter registration efforts 1961–62. Graduated from Tennessee State in 1962.

Lived in Detroit, then Chicago, raising money for SCLC. Moved to the Bahamas in 1971. Returned to Birmingham in 1979, where she became a district sales manager for Avon, retiring in 1998. Now works as a substitute teacher in the public schools.

It might have been around fifth or sixth grade when I began to protest the way things were. I refused to step aside when walking downtown, when a white person would approach me. In high school, we rode city buses to school, and one day my friends and I threw the "colored" sign out the window.

Later, during the sit-ins and picketing in 1960, it was touchy to have someone maybe push you and to not push back. I was Christian and everything, but I was kind of used to pushing back, used to not stepping to the side. With the nonviolence, you're kind of stepping to the side.

I can remember in one of the demonstrations, a white fella with a cigarette coming toward my face. I was just standing there and I was not gonna move. My girlfriend, Lucretia [Collins], was behind me. She told me later that she was gonna put her hand in front of my face. He didn't put the cigarette on me, but I had planned, in my mind, I was gonna stand there.

Photographed
March 25, 2007
Birmingham, AL
Age: 67

WILLIAM HARBOUR

- - - - - - - - -

My mother sent me a letter, after the Freedom Rides.
My mother said, "Son, you can't come home now." It was two and a half years before I could go home to see my family.

My parents had to take the phone out of their house. People would call and say, "Where is the nigger? This nigger's gonna get killed." It worried my mother to death.

I was well known in the community. I was the salutatorian of my high school. Everybody knew me, even the bank. I used to take money to the bank for the school, pick up books for the school, all this for the school. Small hometown.

My father was a supervisor at one of the factories there, so he had hired a lot of folks. They used to ask my father, "What's wrong with that boy?" He said, "Well, no. He finished high school. I sent him to college. He's on his own."

There were cars sitting down the road from the house, and it used to frighten my mother to death all the time.

Photographed
May 8, 2007
Atlanta, GA
Age: 65

BORN
January 9, 1942, in Piedmont, AL, and grew up there.

THEN
Freshman, Tennessee State, Nashville; active in the Nashville Student Movement.

SINCE THEN
Graduated from Tennessee State in 1964. Taught for several years, first in public schools in Blakely, GA, and then with the federal Jobs Corps program in Grants Pass, OR, and Harper's Ferry, WV.

In 1969, moved to Atlanta to work for the federal Office of Economic Opportunity, managing community programs. In 1984, went to work for the army as a civilian management analyst. Retired in 1988. Still active locally in community programs, especially in creating college scholarships.

POLICE DEPT.
JACKSON, MISS
20902

TRAILWAYS

MAY 28

Nashville to Montgomery to Jackson

Allen Cason, Jr.
20914 Nashville, TN - Age 19

Albert Lee Dunn
20917 Clarkston, GA - Age 26 – Died 2005

David Fankhauser
20916 Wilberforce, OH - Age 19

Franklin Hunt
20915 Nashville, TN - Age 22

Larry Hunter
20911 Nashville, TN - Age 18

Pauline Knight-Ofosu
20913 Nashville, TN - Age 20

William Mahoney
20912 Washington, DC - Age 19

David Myers
20910 Wilberforce, OH - Age 21

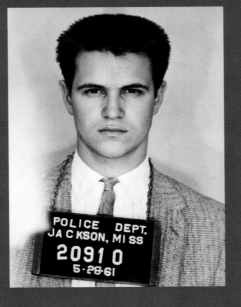

DAVID FANKHAUSER

**I make no bones about it —
I'm not a courageous person.**
Who do you get to go to war? You get the
nineteen-year-olds. They don't have any
idea of what they're getting into. "Well,
they're not really gonna kill me, are
they?" That's not to say I wasn't scared.
I was scared witless.

Before I went to Jackson I went home
and shaved off my beard. My mom gave
me a haircut. I know she was worried,
but she was proud—just like mothers
are proud when their sons go off to war.
They hope for the best, but they're proud
of them doing what they see as a duty.

BORN
November 22, 1941, in Ft. Wayne, IN. Grew up there and in Muncie and
Cincinnati. His stepfather was imprisoned several times for refusing the draft.
His stepfather and mother were members of the Fellowship of Reconcilliation
and active on racial issues. They intentionally lived below the poverty line to
avoid paying "war taxes."

THEN
Student, Central State University, Wilberforce, OH.

SINCE THEN
Graduated from Earlham College, in Richmond, IN, in 1963. Active in civil
rights demonstrations in Cincinnati, later in Vietnam anti-war demonstrations.
Got a Ph.D. in biology from Johns Hopkins in 1971. Since 1973 has been a
professor of chemistry and biology at Clermont College at the University
of Cincinnati.

Photographed
November 18, 2006
Cincinnati, OH
Age: 64

LARRY HUNTER

- - - - - - - - - -

In Parchman I was on the backside of the maximum security unit. We could tell time. There was a barn out back we could see, and we would tell time by the shadow of the boards on the building.

When you're in a maximum security prison like that, the only thing that you look forward to is eating. That's the only thing you look forward to. You know, "When is the next meal?"

"It's five boards 'til the next meal."

BORN
October 2, 1942, in Atlanta and grew up there.

THEN
Student, Tennessee State, in Nashville; active in the Nashville student movement.

SINCE THEN
For several years, alternated SNCC work with college, organizing in Albany, GA, and in Pine Bluff, AR, and attending Fort Valley State College, in Fort Valley, GA.

In 1968 drafted and denied conscientious objector status. Fled to Canada, where he lived in Montreal until returning the United States in 1976. On his return, all charges against him were dropped.

Today he lives in Atlanta and works for the county drivers' education program.

Photographed
May 8, 2007
Atlanta, GA
Age: 64

PAULINE KNIGHT-OFOSU

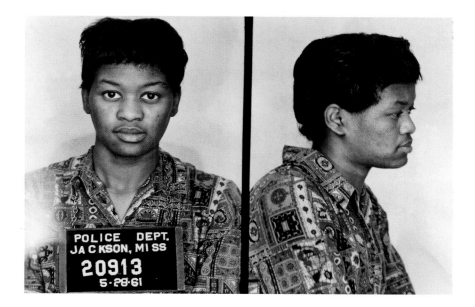

BORN

October 26, 1940, in Nashville, and grew up there.

THEN

Junior, Tennessee State, Nashville; active in the Nashville Student Movement.

SINCE THEN

Graduated Tennessee State in 1962, then from the St. Vincent School of Medical Technology in Indianapolis, IN, the next year. Moved to Washington, DC, in 1964, working as a lab technician and teaching lab techniques at Howard University. Moved to Atlanta in 1968 and ran the labs in the VA hospital.

Joined the EPA in 1972 as its first female pesticide inspector. Later helped prepare civil and criminal cases for pesticide and hazardous substances violations, and trained waste management workers in environmental health issues. Also developed an environmental health curriculum for Clark Atlanta University and taught there for a few years. Now retired and lives in Rex, GA.

My parents never tried to hide anything, but they were strong Bible students, and they would rehearse to you the various things that had happened to people along the way since time began. It wasn't a matter of being afraid—it was a matter of knowing who you were, going forward, and participating with other people and never to hate.

That was something I remember—you cannot hate, you cannot hold this person in error. You've got to see them for who they are. They don't know it, maybe, but they're God's children too. It was that kind of thing that really gave you the strength and brought you forward.

I wasn't afraid. The training that we had gave everybody the conviction that "You can kill my body, but you can't kill my soul." That is a very strong and powerful thing. There really isn't any death, you know—the material body doesn't really constitute death, because it's the idea that counts. This was very important.

Photographed
May 7, 2007
Rex, GA
Age: 66

DAVID MYERS & WINONAH BEAMER

When I was arrested, a reporter from the *Noblesville Daily Ledger,* my hometown paper, did a story on me, with a picture on the front page, a very nice article. The day after my arrest was Memorial Day. The chairman of my draft board was the commander of the American Legion Post and was also the main speaker on the courthouse steps for Memorial Day services, and he lashed out at the newspaper for making a hero of a known communist. I was a communist because I was a conscientious objector—that was his reasoning.

Then they passed a public resolution, which said that I, being a communist, should never be allowed to teach school in the state of Indiana. They sent that on to the governor, Matthew Welsh. Well, the governor later helped pay my bail in Mississippi, so you can see how much credence he gave that.
—David Myers

BORN

David was born February 29, 1940, in Noblesville, IN, and grew up there. Winonah was born September 10, 1941, in Cleveland, and grew up there.

THEN

Both students at Central State University, in Wilberforce, OH.

SINCE THEN

They married in April 1962. David worked as a photographer for several years, first at Central State, then for newspapers in Xenia, OH, and Waterloo, IA. In 1970 worked for three years as the sports information director at Central State. Then worked until 2002 as a photographer, reporter, editor, and producer for WHIO-TV in Dayton, OH.

Winonah spent most of her career working with profoundly retarded adolescents and adults at a number of institutions in Ohio, including twenty-two years with the Montgomery County Board of Mental Retardation.

They now live in Ellenton, FL. Winonah works part-time as a toll-taker on the Sunshine Skyway bridge, which crosses Tampa Bay. David works part-time for the county Mediterranean fruit-fly containment program.

Photographed
April 30, 2007
Ellenton, FL
Ages: 67 and 65

MAY | JUN | JUL | AUG | SEP

ILLINOIS CENTRAL TRAIN STATION

MAY 30

New Orleans to Jackson

James Davis, Jr.
20918 Orangeburg, SC - Age 21 - Died 2006

Charles Haynie
20920 Ithaca, NY - Age 25 - Died 2001

Glenda Gaither
20923 Orangeburg, SC - Age 18

Robert Heller
20919 New Orleans, LA - Age 19

Paul Green
20921 Ithaca, NY - Age 22

Sandra Nixon
20922 New Orleans, LA - Age 19

Joe Griffith
20924 Ithaca, NY - Age 26

Peter Sterling
20925 Ithaca, NY - Age 20

TRAILWAYS

JUNE 2

Montgomery to Jackson

Charles Butler
20929 Nashville, TN - Age 18 - Died 2000

Joy Reagon
20930 Nashville, TN - Age 19

Price Chatham
20932 East Rockaway, NY - Age 29

Kenneth Shilman
20933 Oceanside, NY - Age 18 - Died 1989

Joseph McDonald
20931 Oceanside, NY - Age 20

Ruby Doris Smith
20928 Atlanta, GA - Age 19 - Died 1967

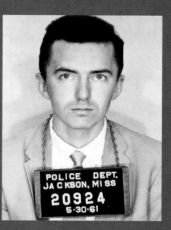

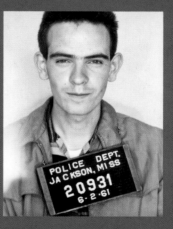

ROBERT HELLER

I always felt safe and part of the reason I felt safe was I really thought that the Kennedys were watching us all the time. I really felt that. Probably totally untrue but that's the way I felt. I felt the world was watching us. I couldn't imagine anybody doing anything to hurt us in prison.

After I bailed out, I went back to New York, back to my parents' house in Rockville Centre. I remember being interviewed by the *New York Times* and the local paper, *Newsday.* I remember not really wanting this to be my life. I was kind of annoyed about all the publicity. I wanted to get out. I just decided to leave and go to San Francisco and didn't tell anybody there I was involved in the Freedom Rides.

As far as I was concerned, it was too much attention for the wrong reason. I felt like I didn't do anything special. I just added my body to a movement. It wasn't anything intellectual. I didn't discover anything. I didn't do anything heroic.

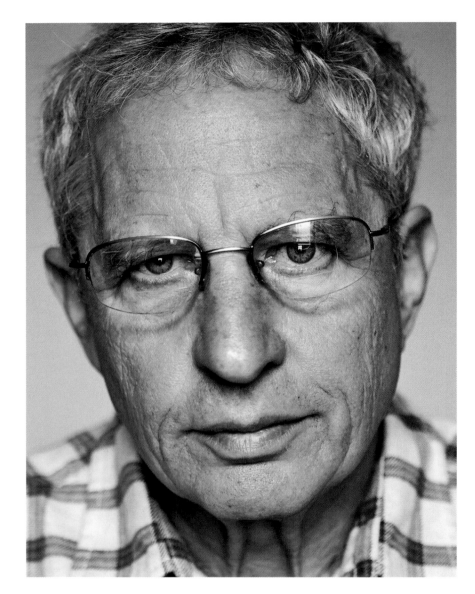

BORN

February 17, 1942, in Philadelphia. Grew up in Brooklyn, Queens, and Rockville Centre, NY.

THEN

Sophomore, Tulane University. Active member of CORE in New Orleans.

SINCE THEN

Lived in San Francisco for a year, working as a longshoreman. Returned to Tulane for another year, then dropped out to work as an announcer and cinematographer for a local TV station. Moved to New York in 1965 and began making industrial films, working for production companies until 1979, then advertising agencies, including Ogilvy & Mather. Retired in 1986 and works on occasional projects.

Photographed
October 24, 2007
New York, NY
Age: 65

PETER STERLING

BORN
June 28, 1940, in Manhattan. Grew up in Queens and in Rye, NY.

THEN
Junior at Cornell University, Ithaca, NY

SINCE THEN
Earned a Ph.D. in biology at Case Western Reserve University in Cleveland in the mid-sixties. Active with the local CORE chapter. Post-doctorate work in the late 1960s at Harvard; while there, protested against the Vietnam War and counseled draftees who wanted to become conscientious objectors.

Since 1980 has been a professor of neuroscience at the University of Pennsylvania School of Medicine. Has also used his scientific training to pursue social issues. He has studied the neural processes by which racial and economic conditions can adversely affect people's health, and how electroshock therapy and psychoactive drugs can damage the brain. He has testified numerous times on behalf of patients.

Before we left, I called my father. He had certainly seen those photos in the newspapers and on TV. He had followed all the Southern travesties since the Scottsboro boys. So when I called to tell him I was going, he certainly knew the danger. He was calm and supportive. He didn't try to persuade me otherwise.

Years later, when I was in my forties, I got interested in Judaism, and I read the Old Testament for the first time, and of course I read about Abraham and Isaac, and I was stunned to see Abraham risking everything with his son for his commitment.

But a bigger jolt came about six months later, when I mentioned this insight to my father. I asked if he had realized in 1961, when I called to tell him I was going, that we were replaying Abraham and Isaac. He'd been raised an atheist and rigorously nonobservant Jew, so it was a fair question. There was a moment of silence and then a choked, "yes." That was when I felt the story's full power—a man must have values; he must teach them to his son—but then he must live in silence with their terrifying consequences.

Photographed
June 1, 2007
Philadelphia, PA
Age: 66

PRICE CHATHAM

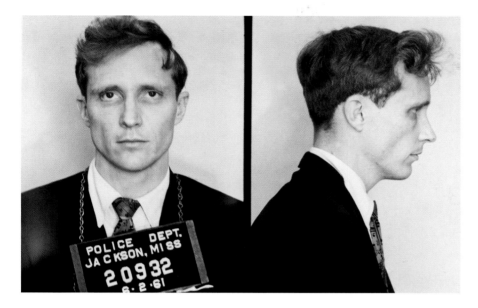

BORN
June 5, 1931, in New Gulf, TX, and grew up there. Attended college at Tulane, in New Orleans, and St. John's, in Annapolis, MD.

THEN
Married with a child, living in East Rockaway, NY, working as a script reader for Paramount Pictures.

SINCE THEN
Has worked as a freelance writer and also owned a café in the East Village for a number of years. Now retired and lives in Manhattan.

In Parchman, they would ask different people to lead the prayers.
This Quaker in my cell volunteered to lead the prayer. And he spent all day long working on those prayers, prancing up and down the cell, dear heavenly father and all the bullshit. I got so sick of this stuff.

Finally, I said, "Well, I'll lead the prayer." Some of them didn't like it. Some of the militant blacks didn't like the idea that Price was going to lead the prayer. The subject of my prayer was: dear heavenly Father, please help us to hate our jailers more. We don't want to love our jailers, we want to hate them.

When I finished this prayer one of the priests calls out, "Brother So-and-so, do you accept that prayer?" And he said, "No, I do not accept that prayer." So they decided only professionals from then on would be allowed to lead the prayers.

Photographed
June 20, 2006
New York, NY
Age: 75

TRAILWAYS

JUNE 2

Montgomery to Jackson

Richard Gleason
20934 Chicago, IL - Age 24

Jesse J. Harris
20940 Washington, DC - Age 24

Cordell Reagon
20935 Nashville, TN - Age 18 - Died 1996

Carolyn Reed
20936 Nashville, TN - Age 21

Felix Singer
20938 Chicago, IL - Age 32

Leslie Word
20939 Corinth, MS - Age 28

Elizabeth Wykcoff
20937 New York, NY - Age 45 - Died 1994

TRAILWAYS

JUNE 6

New Orleans to Jackson

Johnny Ashford
20954 Chicago, IL - Age 22

Abraham Bassford IV
20955 Brooklyn, NY - Age 24

James McDonough
20949 Toronto, ON - Age 22

Terry Sullivan
20950 Chicago, IL - Age 23

Shirley Thompson
20952 New Orleans, LA - Age 18 - Died 1999

James Wahlstrom
20953 Madison, WI - Age 24

Ernest Weber
20951 East Orange, NJ - Age 52 - Died 2003

ABRAHAM BASSFORD IV

POLICE DEPT.
JACKSON, MISS
20955
6·6·61

I remember when I hit jail, the first thing I was told was, we're fasting to the death. Oh, death is not that attractive, and I didn't know whether I wanted to fast until then or till segregation is ended. Yes, I said, well, you're dreaming. We have a decent cause and we shouldn't be in jail, and fasting is an appropriate witness objection. I'll join you in the fast as long as I can hold out.

So for about twenty-one days I fasted, and then for another seven days after that. But after twenty-eight days, I said the heck with it.

Photographed
September 16, 2006
Chicago, IL
Age: 69

BORN

October 16, 1936, in Manhattan. Grew up there and in Brooklyn, NY. In 1956, as a college freshman, registered as a conscientious objector. Joined the Socialist Party in 1958 and CORE in 1960.

THEN

Student, Wagner College, Staten Island.

SINCE THEN

In the mid-sixties studied at New York Theological Seminary and ran the Student Peace Union, a national organization; worked in training in several churches in New York. Chaplain at the Methodist Hospital in Brooklyn in the late 1960s.

Quit the Socialist Party in 1968 over its support of the Vietnam War; later rejoined and served as the party's national secretary for four years in the mid-seventies. Returned to the seminary, this time at Garrett Evangelical Theological Seminary in Evanston, IL, where he studied for four years in the late 1970s and early 1980s. Now retired and living in Chicago.

JAMES WAHLSTROM

Photographed
February 21, 2007
Grants Pass, OR
Age: 70

When I came back to Wisconsin I was kind of like a celebrity.

I didn't come back thinking, "Well, I'm gonna try and get six or seven of my friends to go" or "I'm gonna have a campus rally tonight." I wasn't really an agitator. I was just a foot soldier. And I realized that somehow I had left the front lines.

I felt it like it wasn't about social celebrity or becoming somebody's role model. It really was important to fill up the jails.

The second time I went down to Mississippi, I was all alone. I got off the bus and I had been traveling for — I don't know. I was tired. I was crazy.

I knew the bus station and I knew the routine. I walked in and a cop followed me in when I went into the "colored" section and into a phone booth. He knocked on the door of the booth and said, "Boy, what are you doing?"

"I'm calling my lawyer," I said. Of course, I didn't have a lawyer.

BORN
October 30, 1936, in Milwaukee, WI, and grew up there.

THEN
Junior, University of Wisconsin, in Madison. Had joined the Army in 1957, after his first two years of college at the University of Wisconsin in Milwaukee. Served twenty-one months in Kansas and Alaska. In early 1961 had visited Cuba on a trip sponsored by the Fair Play for Cuba Committee.

SINCE THEN
After being released from Parchman and returning to Madison, came back on his own and was arrested a second time as a Freedom Rider, again in the Greyhound station, on July 31st. He bailed out on September 9th.

Studied for a year at University of California at Berkeley, then returned to school in Wisconsin. Dropped out and moved to New York City for a year, then to San Francisco, working at various jobs in both cities. Was involved in the Free Speech movement at Berkeley and anti-war protests.

In 1969 moved with his wife and three children to a farm in southwestern Oregon that had once been a homestead. Since the early 1990s has lived in nearby Grants Pass, OR.

TRAILWAYS

JUNE 7

Nashville to Jackson

John Gager
20958 New Haven, CT - Age 23

Rev. Reginald Green
20962 Richmond, VA - Age 21

Ed Kale
20957 New Haven, CT - Age 24

Raymond Randolph, Jr.
20961 Richmond, VA - Age 21

Carol Silver
20959 New York, NY - Age 22

Obadiah Simms III
20960 Richmond, VA - Age 21 - Died 2000

GREYHOUND

JUNE 7

Jackson

Michael Audain
20968 Vancouver, BC - Age 23

HAWKINS FIELD, JACKSON AIRPORT

JUNE 7

St. Louis to Jackson

Gwendolyn Jenkins
20963 St. Louis, MO - Age 21

Robert Jenkins
20964 St. Louis, MO - Age 27 - Died 1979

Ralph Washington
20965 St. Louis, MO - Age 24 - Died 1981

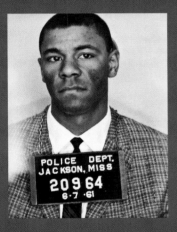

JOHN GAGER

- - - - - - - - -

The greatest influence on me to go on the Freedom Rides was Bill Coffin, who was then the chaplain at Yale, and who was part of the Freedom Rides in Alabama. [Coffin was arrested at the Greyhound station in Birmingham on May 25th].

He came back and said, "You know, this is our struggle. It's not just about the South. It's a struggle in which all of us are involved."

He said that we have an obligation to support them, to become involved, to become engaged and make ourselves available to do what we can under their leadership. It never was that white folks in the North are going to go down and save these benighted Negroes in the South. It was that SNCC and CORE and Martin Luther King were leading us.

BORN

November 21, 1937, in Boston. Grew up in various places in New England. Attended Phillips Exeter Academy, in Exeter, NH, and Yale University, in New Haven, CT, where he was active in civil rights demonstrations.

THEN

Student at Yale Divinity School.

SINCE THEN

Finished at Yale Divinity in 1962. Active in New Haven in civil rights efforts. Studied in Europe for two years, then got his Ph.D. in religion at Harvard.

Taught at Princeton from 1968 until he retired in 2006; a professor of religion, his focus was on early Christianity and early Judaism. Among his books are *Kingdom and Community: The Social World of Early Christianity* and *The Origins of Anti-Semitism: Attitudes toward Judaism in Pagan and Christian Antiquity.*

Photographed
June 14, 2007
Princeton, NJ
Age: 69

REV. REGINALD GREEN

I never asked my father and mother if I could go on the Freedom Rides, for fear that they would say no. Out of respect I would have honored their direction. Rather than have to face that, I just decided that I would go.

My dad found out from a reporter from the *Evening Star*, who somehow got a list of names of who had been arrested. It showed persons in this area and he obviously came across my name. He called my father and asked him if he had a son named Reginald Green at Virginia Union. My father said yes, but that I would not be home this summer because I was in Richmond working and preparing to return to school in September.

That's when the reporter was nice enough to say, "I'd like to come and see you," rather than just tell him over the phone. My father thought, this is unusual, a white reporter wanting to sit down with a black man in his neighborhood. The reporter came out and told him that I was in jail in Mississippi. That's how he found out. Two days later he he got a letter from me.

BORN
June 17, 1939, in Washington, DC, and grew up there.

THEN
Sophomore at Virginia Union University, in Richmond.

SINCE THEN
Returned to Virginia Union, graduating in 1964 and then again in 1967 with a degree in theology. He moved back to DC, and was pastor at Walker Memorial Baptist Church until he retired in 2006. From 1968 to 1990 he also worked as an administrator for the DC housing and development agency.

Photographed
May 30, 2007
Washington, DC
Age: 67

ED KALE

BORN

January 16, 1937, in Des Moines, IA. Grew up primarily in Grangeville, ID.

THEN

Student, Yale Divinity School. Had done his undergraduate work at the University of Idaho, in Moscow, and Denver University.

SINCE THEN

Taught at the American colleges in Instanbul, Turkey, and Athens, Greece, for three years, then finished at Yale Divinity in 1965. Briefly led a church in Connecticut, then left to study at Durham University, in England, in 1966. Very active in the United States and England in the anti-war movement.

Served as the chaplain at Liverpool University in England and then at Mainz University in Germany. Returned to the United States in 1978, and taught at the University of Idaho. Served as the campus minister and taught at the University of Texas, Arlington, and the University of Minnesota, Duluth. Active in the anti-apartheid movement, in support of human rights in Central America, and against Star Wars.

Since 2004 has lived in La Pointe, WI, on Madeline Island in Lake Superior, where he runs a kayak rental business.

Carol [Silver] and I have talked about this quite often because we were awfully naïve—idealistic and naïve. Our bus made a stop just before we got to Jackson. And I thought, "Oh well, I'll just go get a couple of postcards to send to my parents and friends." I went out there wearing a windbreaker with the Yale logo. You can see it in my mug shot.

About ten, fifteen feet from the bus I was surrounded by a group of whites. It scared the hell out of me because— and I remember the exact words— "What the hell you doing down here, Yankee!" The bus driver, bless him, reached out, grabbed me, pulled me in and drove off.

Later, in Parchman, I played the religious card to the nth degree. I said, "You know I realize this is a God-fearing state and so forth, could we have Bibles?" We didn't want Bibles necessarily to read them. We wanted page number one—the blank page— to make our chess sets. So they gave us Bibles and we made our chess sets and we'd sit there by the hour. That's all we had. Without those chess sets, we would have gone bonkers.

Photographed
November 10, 2006
La Pointe, WI
Age: 69

CAROL SILVER

The ride between Jackson and Parchman took about four hours and was more frightening than any previous part of the jail experience. There were twenty-three girls, white and black, crowded into an army transport-type truck, which was completely lacking in springs. Many of us had black-and-blue marks when we arrived, because the drivers delighted in stopping and starting suddenly, throwing us against each other and the sharp corners of the seats.

But the most terrifying part of the ride was the three times when the driver suddenly jolted off to the side of the highway and stopped. We imagined every horror, including an ambush by the KKK. I suppose they were just waiting for our escort of state police and FBI to catch up, or something equally innocent, but until we were moving again, none of us breathed an easy breath.

BORN
Born October 1, 1938, in Boston, MA, and grew up there and in Revere and and Worcester.

THEN
Living in New York and working at the United Nations. Graduated from the University of Chicago in 1960.

SINCE THEN
Attended law school at the University of Chicago. Organized a chapter of the Law Students Civil Rights Research Council, which supported civil rights lawyers working in the South with summer interns and research. After graduating law school in 1964, interned for a year with Floyd McKissick, a prominent black attorney in North Carolina.

From 1965 to 1970, worked in federal programs in various cities in California providing legal services for the poor, returning each summer to Mississippi and Louisiana to work with the Lawyers Constitutional Defense Committee.

Elected to three terms on the San Francisco Board of Supervisors, serving from 1977 to 1989. Since then has practiced law in San Francisco. In 2002 started the Afghan Friends Network, to aid in Afghan redevelopment.

Photographed
February 18, 2007
San Francisco, CA
Age: 66

MICHAEL AUDAIN

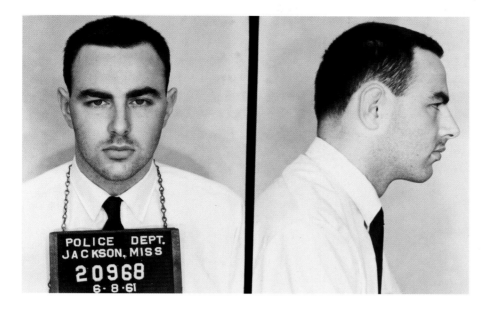

POLICE DEPT.
JACKSON, MISS
20968
6·8·61

BORN

July 31, 1937, in Bournemouth, England. Grew up in Victoria, British Columbia. A fifth-generation British Columbian, his great-grandfather, James Dunsmuir, had been a prominent industrialist and politician in the province.

THEN

Had finished his third year at the University of British Columbia, in Vancouver. One of the few Freedom Riders arrested in Jackson who came alone, without working through organizers.

SINCE THEN

Helped found the British Columbia Civil Liberties Association in 1962. Graduated from the University of British Columbia in 1963, then did graduate studies there. Active in the nuclear-disarmament movement. Studied at the London School of Economics 1966-68, then moved to Toronto. Active in the anti-Vietnam War movement in London and Toronto.

In 1980, started Polygon Homes, a residential real estate development company, in Vancouver, which he still runs today. Active as a philanthropist in the arts. A member of the British Columbia Arts Council and a trustee of the National Gallery of Canada.

The Jackson police didn't have to arrest me, but since they did, fine.

I was so delighted to meet the other Freedom Riders in jail. In many ways, the experience changed my life.

When I came back to Canada, I helped start the BC Civil Liberties Association. I got involved in the peace movement. I was president of the Nuclear Disarmament Club at UBC and organized peace marches and sit-ins for peace.

Later, I was involved with Vietnam War resistance in eastern Canada and in England. In May, 1968, I was sent as a delegate from the London School of Economics to the general strike in Paris. I was at Woodstock — I was living in a commune in Toronto at the time.

I was involved in a lot of stuff, but it all stemmed from the Freedom Riders. I'd never really been politically involved before.

Photographed
February 26, 2007
Vancouver, BC
Age: 69

HAWKINS FIELD, JACKSON AIRPORT

JUNE 8

Montgomery to Jackson

Mark Lane
20970 New York, NY - Age 34

Percy Sutton
20969 New York, NY - Age 40

ILLINOIS CENTRAL TRAIN STATION

JUNE 8

New Orleans to Jackson

Travis Britt
20979 Washington, DC - Age 27

Jan Triggs
20976 Washington, DC - Age 19

Stokely Carmichael
20978 New York, NY - Age 19 - Died 1998

Joan Trumpauer Mulholland
20975 Washington, DC - Age 19

Gwendolyn Greene
20971 Washington, DC - Age 19

Rev. Robert Wesby
20977 Washington, DC - Age 18 - Died 1988

Teri Perlman
20974 New York, NY - Age 19

Helen Wilson
20972 Washington, DC - Age 26

Jane Rosett
20973 Washington, DC - Age 18

ILLINOIS CENTRAL TRAIN STATION

JUNE 9

Nashville to Jackson

Winonah Beamer
20980 Wilberforce, OH - Age 19

Del Greenblatt
20981 Ithaca, NY - Age 21

Edward Bromberg
20983 New York, NY - Age 27 - Died 2001

Heath Rush
20984 Wilberforce, OH - Age 20

Patricia Bryant
20982 Wilberforce, OH - Age 20

POLICE DEPT.
JACKSON, MISS
20975
6-8-61

JOAN TRUMPAUER MULHOLLAND

Photographed
July 26, 2007
Arlington, VA
Age: 65

We were transferred to Parchman in a van or maybe a paddy wagon. There were only women on the trip, and it might have just been white women. At some point, the driver pulled off on some dirt road and stopped at some house back in the woods. Which, of course, made us think that we might all be killed.

Probably he needed to make a pit stop and wanted to show off to his friends, "Lookie what I got!" But at the time, it was like, "Oh, God!" [*Laughs.*] There were guys looking in, probably trying to intimidate us a little bit. In reality, I expect it was a pit stop. But I remember that as being one of those moments where you make peace with the Almighty.

Then it was night, I think, when we got to Parchman—getting processed and a change of clothes and vaginal searches. The matrons would dip their—as I recollect, it was gloved hands, but somebody else may remember it differently—they would dip 'em into these buckets of whatever between gouging up us. It smelled like Lysol or Pine-Sol, one of those highly disinfectant things. It was all frightening. I think it was meant to impress the seriousness of our isolation and they could do anything they wanted to.

BORN

September 14, 1941, in Washington, DC. Grew up in Arlington and Fairfax, VA.

THEN

Living in Arlington and working on Capitol Hill, active with the Nonviolent Action Group protesting in Washington, northern Virginia, and Maryland. Had studied for one year at Duke University; active in picketing and sit-ins in Durham, NC.

SINCE THEN

Transferred to Tougaloo College in Jackson, MS, and graduated in 1964; stayed active in the movement while in school.

In 1964 returned to Arlington, where she has since lived. Worked for the Smithsonian, then for a federal program helping communities resolve racial issues. From 1980 until her retirement in 2007, worked as an assistant teacher in the Arlington public schools.

GREYHOUND

JUNE 10

Nashville to Jackson

Leora Berman
20993 Chicago, IL - Age 18

Stephen Green
20994 Middlebury, VT - Age 21

Richard Griswold
20992 Brooklyn, NY - Age 34

Leon Horne
20990 Chicago, IL - Age 24

Katherine Pleune
20991 Chicago, IL - Age 21

Lewell Woods, Jr.
20989 Chicago, IL - Age 34 - Died 1998

LIVINGSTON PARK

JUNE 10

Jackson

Amos Brown
20987 Jackson, MS - Age 20

James Hopkins
20986 Jackson, MS - Age 19

GREYHOUND

JUNE 11

Nashville to Jackson

Zev Aelony
21000 Minneapolis, MN - Age 23

Robert Baum
20995 Minneapolis, MN - Age 19

Marv Davidov
20996 Minneapolis, MN - Age 29

David Morton
20999 Minneapolis, MN - Age 21

Claire O'Connor
20997 Minneapolis, MN - Age 22

Gene Uphoff
20998 Minneapolis, MN - Age 19

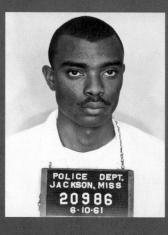

STEPHEN GREEN

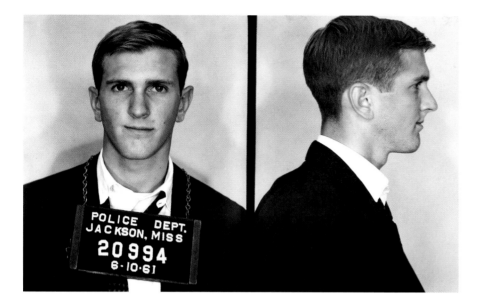

POLICE DEPT.
JACKSON, MISS
20994
6·10·61

In Parchman, I was in a cell next to Stokely Carmichael. I was young and full of excitement about what was happening. The school year had just ended, and one day I said, "All those college students are going to come to Mississippi!"

From the next cell over, I hear Stokely say: "Hear that, everybody? The white boys and girls from Harvard and Yale are going to come save us!" [*Laughs.*]

BORN
May 22, 1940, in Muncie, IN. Grew up primarily in Louisville, KY, and Elmira, NY.

THEN
Junior at Middlebury College, in Middlebury, VT.

SINCE THEN
Graduated Middlebury in 1962 and served two years in Niger in the Peace Corps. Since then has worked extensively for the United Nations and its various agencies, including UNICEF and the World Food Program, in hot spots around the world. Was the deputy country director for UNICEF in Ethiopia 1973–76, where he helped expose and then respond to the famine the government of Haile Selassie was trying to conceal. Has served in Somalia, Darfur, Angola, and the Balkans, as well as other locations.

Has also worked as a journalist, and written two books about the relationship between the United States and Israel. From 2004–06, served a term as a representative in the Vermont state legislature. He lives in Berlin, VT.

Photographed
May 14, 2005
Berlin, VT
Age: 64

ZEV AELONY

We were riding in a car, and the state patrolman who was driving it said, "You know, I got nothing against colored, but this mixing just doesn't work."

We're sitting in the back of this car with this guy with a gun, and not all that interested in ending up dead by the side of the road. Neither of us, I think, said anything.

The patrolman said, "I know because of the tragedy in my own family. Yeah, one of my uncles, he was in the Army in World War II. He inter-married and came back, and it's never been the same for our family."

We're sitting there wondering what's — you know, if he'd been in North Africa, maybe he married an African woman, and he couldn't come back to Mississippi. So we're sitting there, and he said, "Yeah, every time we have a family reunion, you know it's not polite to not eat some of what everybody brings."

And he said, "You can't believe how bad it is to have to eat that Latvian food. [*Laughs.*] We've all been suffering."

Photographed
November 4, 2006
Angora, MN
Age: 68

BORN

February 21, 1938, in Palo Alto, CA. Grew up in Dayton, OH, and in Minneapolis.

THEN

Senior at the University of Minnesota, in Minneapolis. In 1958 lived on a kibbutz in Israel. In 1959 lived at Koinonia Farm, a radical Christian commune in Georgia, then attended a nonviolence training session run by CORE. When he returned to the university in the fall of 1959, he helped start Students for Integration.

SINCE THEN

From 1962–65, worked for CORE as a member of Soul Force, a national team that worked with local chapters and other civil rights groups around the country. Arrested frequently, and twice beaten severely in jail, once in Ocala, FL, and once in Americus, GA. In 1963, he was arrested in Americus and charged with sedition under an 1871 law, possibly facing the death penalty. Was held in jail for four months, along with three others similarly charged, until a federal court dismissed the charges.

Taught college for a few years, then ran an industrial electronics business in Los Angeles. Returned to Minneapolis in 1976 and went to work as a manufacturers' representative for companies making industrial electronic equipment, which he still does part-time today. Remains active in local politics.

GENE UPHOFF

BORN

April 3, 1942, in Prairie du Sac, WI. Grew up on a farm near Oregon, WI, and in Minneapolis. The farm, owned by the Fellowship of Reconciliation and run by his parents, served as a retreat for conscientious objectors and activists. His father was a conscientious objector who ran for the U.S. Senate as a socialist in 1944.

THEN

Junior, University of Minnesota. Had registered as a conscientious objector. Active in Students for Integration and the Student Peace Union.

SINCE THEN

Graduated Minnesota, then went to medical school at the University of Colorado. Has practiced family medicine ever since, first in public clinics in Denver and, since 1973, in Portland, OR. Today runs a private family clinic; his practice includes a significant percentage of patients with Medicaid or no insurance.

Photographed
February 24, 2007
Portland, OR
Age: 64

ROBERT BAUM

BORN

March 6, 1942, in East Orange, NJ. Grew up in Palos Heights, IL, and Minneapolis.

THEN

Student, University of Minnesota, Minneapolis. Member of Students for Integration.

SINCE THEN

Lived in New York City for a year. Returned to Minneapolis, and alternatively worked and continued his studies in at the university. Active in protests against the Vietnam War. From 1972 to 1991 worked as a custodian for the university. Since 1995 he has been a bus driver there.

Photographed
November 6, 2006
Minneapolis, MN
Age: 64

MARV DAVIDOV

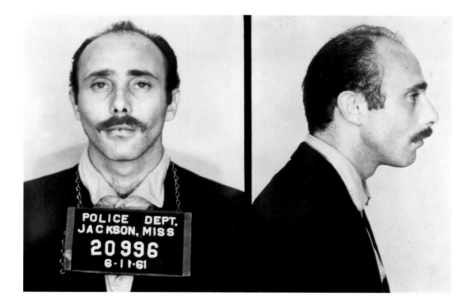

BORN

August 26, 1931, in Detroit and grew up there. Moved in 1949 with his family to St. Paul, MN. Drafted into the army in 1953 before his senior year at Macalester College, in St. Paul, and served nineteen months.

THEN

Art dealer, activist, and organizer in Minneapolis.

SINCE THEN

Took part in a seventeen-month Canada-to-Cuba Peace Walk 1963–64. Active in the mid-sixties in the antiwar and draft resistance movements in Berkeley and Los Angeles.

Returned to Minneapolis in 1968 and began the Honeywell Project, which he would run for the next twenty-two years. The project's goal was to force Honeywell, a Minneapolis-based company, to stop making cluster bombs, land mines, and other weapons. Honeywell spun off its weapons business into a new company in 1990.

Has organized on behalf of a wide range of groups, including the American Indian Movement, farmers, and hotel workers. Has taught a course on active nonviolence at the University of St. Thomas, in St. Paul, since 1992. Started a local chapter of the War Resisters League in 2006.

After we were arrested, we met Jack Young, our attorney, who was black. "You're gonna be tried today. It'll take that jury fifteen minutes to convict you. [Capt. J. L.] Ray [the arresting officer] is gonna lie and blacks do not sit on juries. Women don't. You're gonna get Baptists, maybe a Methodist or a Presbyterian. Catholics don't sit on juries. No Jews."

Sure enough, eleven Baptists and one Presbyterian on our jury. Capt. Ray came in and lied, saying, "It was an angry, hostile mob there, so to protect them I had to arrest them on breach of the peace," which I thought was a marvelous charge.

What's their peace? Segregation, lynchings, brutality, unemployment, poor schooling, poor nutrition, South Africa apartheid town. We could see the stars and bars flying above the U.S. flag across the street. "Wow. It's *Gone with the Wind.*" [*Laughs.*]

Photographed
November 3, 2006
Minneapolis, MN
Age: 75

DAVID MORTON

- - - - - - - - -

I had a nice apartment, a cute girlfriend, and one day Zev [Aelony] calls me up and says, "Eh, you want to go to jail?" How can I explain? I was raised radical. I'm still a radical. My kids are radicals, trust me. My parents weren't commies but they were radical.

We met on the quad, on the steps. Zev and me and Claire [O'Connor] and so forth. Here comes Marv [Davidov]. He's just walking through the campus, and I wave at him because he's a buddy of mine, okay, once and always. He came over. The next thing you know, he decided to join the rest of us and go get thrown in jail.

Well, what did he do the rest of his life? Political activist. I teased him, I said, "You know, you were just walking by. You had no idea." That became his life's work.

BORN

November 14, 1939, in Salt Lake City, UT. Grew up there, in Berkeley, upstate New York, and St. Paul, MN, where he moved with his family in 1947.

THEN

Folk musician and poet, a dropout from the University of Minnesota and a leading figure on the counterculture scene in Minneapolis. Is credited with giving the first live performance at the legendary coffee house the Ten O'Clock Scholar in 1958, the year it opened. Bob Dylan, John Koerner, and Dave Ray, among many others, were soon playing at the Scholar and other local clubs.

SINCE THEN

Lived in Minneapolis in the sixties but spent much time in Los Angeles, San Francisco, Chicago, and New York, playing music and reading his poetry.

In 1971 moved to northern Minnesota, just outside Angora. Worked as a cement finisher on industrial construction projects until 2001. Now retired, still plays three to four concerts a year with the Duke Savages, a jug band he started in 1964.

Photographed
November 8, 2006
Angora, MN
Age: 66

CLAIRE O'CONNOR

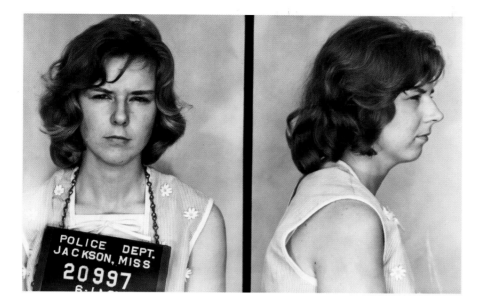

BORN

July 25, 1938, in Boston. Grew up there and in St. Paul, MN.

THEN

Freshman at the University of Minnesota; worked part-time as an LPN at the university hospital.

SINCE THEN

Returned to Mississippi in 1964 during Freedom Summer. Did voter registration work in the northern part of the state until May 1965.

Graduated University of Minnesota in 1966. Moved to Regina, Saskatchewan, in 1971, and worked with an organization counseling inner-city youth and later for another group that helped battered women. In 1993 moved to Winnipeg, Manitoba, where she worked with at-risk families to help prevent child abuse.

Returned to Minneapolis in 1997 and worked as the executive director of a clinic trying to reduce teen pregnancy by providing birth-control information and sex education.

Now retired and lives in Eden Prairie, MN. Remains active in local politics.

In Parchman there was this constant kind of needling from a group of two or three women. They were trustees. They would saunter through and watch us while we were showering. We weren't allowed to smoke, and they'd have cigarettes and they'd flick the ashes at us. That kind of stuff. They were Euro-American not African American.

One of the most difficult things for those who lived in the South to reconcile were the white women Freedom Riders. How do you treat them? They didn't know.

The warden came to greet us on the morning of the second day. He sauntered up and down and said, "Welcome to Parchman." He was really kind of welcoming, just being a good host. He said "We got the best biscuits in Mississippi. Anything ya'll want?"

Some people said, "Yeah, we want something to read."

He said, "You've got the Bible."

At the time we only had the New Testament. We said, "We want the real Bible. We want the Old Testament."

And he said "Oh. Some of ya'll are Jewish. Some of my best friends are Jewish." We just cracked up but we got our Old Testament.

For the record, I read the whole damn book and I have never read the Bible before or since. I didn't read the begats, but I read everything else.

Photographed
November 2, 2006
Eden Prarie, MN
Age: 68

GREYHOUND

JUNE 14

Jackson

Daniel Ray Thompson
21005 Cleveland, OH – Age 26 - Died 2004

GREYHOUND

JUNE 16

Nashville to Jackson

Elizabeth Adler
21013 Madison, WI - Age 21

Bob Filner
21014 Ithaca, NY - Age 18

Elizabeth Hirshfeld
21015 Ithaca, NY - Age 24

Karen Kytle
21016 Oklahoma City, OK - Age 18

Leon Rice
21017 Chicago, IL - Age 24

GREYHOUND

JUNE 19

Jackson

Eugene Levine
21026 Stillwater, OK - Age 34

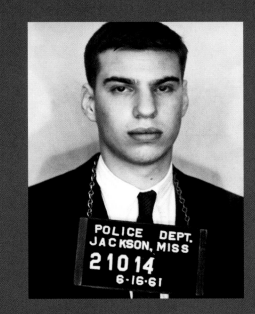

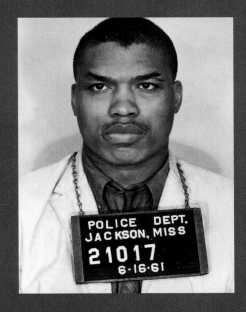

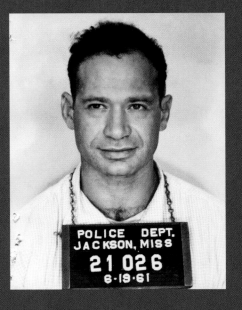

POLICE DEPT.
JACKSON, MISS
21014
6-16-61

BOB FILNER

------- ------- -------

My father used to say, "Well, I didn't mind if he was a Freedom Rider, but did he have to do it on my credit card?" I'd used his credit card to get to Nashville, I guess. Elizabeth Hirshfeld and I flew there.

Once I was in Parchman, the other Freedom Riders determined that my dad had money, so they would make up songs about me. One of the verses for "Keep Your Eyes on the Prize," went, "My father was a member of the bourgeoisie, but I will fight for freedom while he's supporting me."

They did it in sort of a nice—they were saying, "Oh, well, he has money, but he's still with us." But they were also making it clear that I was different.

BORN

September 4, 1942, in Pittsburgh. Grew up there and in Queens, NY. His father was a businessman who raised money for Martin Luther King beginning in the 1950s. In 1957, organized a group of fellow high school students to attend a civil rights march in Washington, DC.

THEN

Sophomore at Cornell University, in Ithaca, NY.

SINCE THEN

Graduated Cornell in 1963, and got a Ph.D. there in 1969 in the history of science. Taught history at San Diego State University from 1970 until 1992, when he won election to the House of Representatives. He continues to represent what is now the state's 51st district, which includes the southern half of San Diego and area to the east.

Photographed
June 26, 2007
Washington, DC
Age: 64

ELIZABETH HIRSHFELD

━ ━ ━ ━ ━ ━ ━ ━ ━

After the Freedom Rides I was in Detroit raising money for CORE. There was an organization in Detroit called Friends of the South and it was kind of an upper-middle-class leftist, Jewish red-diaper-baby organization and they took me under their wing and helped me.

I talked to unions, I talked to churches, I talked to synagogues, I talked to parties. I set up parties when people would come from the South.

I eventually raised $2,000. Two thousand dollars doesn't seem like very much right now, but $2,000 then was a lot. That was my first goal. After that I just raised money for continuing business.

What I did before was to go to the drama department in Ithaca and ask them to help me figure out what to say. The first appearance I had to do was a talk to the election board in Syracuse, NY. A guy from the drama department just said, "Tell me your story." I did and he said, "That's it. That's all you have to do is say that." Then, he just taught me to organize it slightly.

It's a really great story. It was in the news and here's this white innocent young woman, you know, with this dramatic story and they get to see a real Freedom Rider. Actually, it wasn't that hard to raise money.

I raised money all the rest of my life, one form or another, until I started being a teacher.

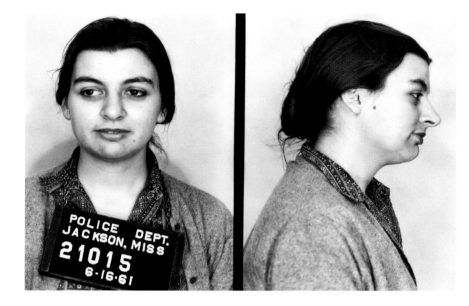

BORN
May 21, 1937, in Ithaca, NY. Grew up in and around Detroit.

THEN
Living in Ithaca, NY, working at a field station of the Atomic Energy Commission. Graduated from Cornell University in 1959.

SINCE THEN
Moved back to Detroit, and raised money for CORE and the Freedom Rides. Worked with the Northern Student Movement, a counterpart to SNCC, doing community organizing around education and employment issues. Also helped run a rent strike in New York City. Lobbied Democratic Party office holders and union officials in Michigan to support the Mississippi Freedom Democratic Party's effort to get seated at the 1964 convention in Atlantic City. Later worked to help organize a chapter of the United Farm Workers Union in Michigan.

Moved to Oakland, CA, in 1969. Worked as a financial planner for ten years for an insurance company. Since 2000 has taught biology and other science courses at John F. Kennedy High School in Richmond, CA.

Photographed
September 7, 2005
Richmond, CA
Age: 68

POLICE DEPT.
JACKSON, MISS
21026
6-19-61

EUGENE LEVINE

I drove straight from Stillwater [OK] to the Jackson train station and got arrested.

The police saw I was alone—I hate joining groups—and older than the usual Freedom Rider. I told them I was a veteran—in the 11th Airborne in postwar Japan—and they said, "We're going to take you back to your car, and you can go home."

I told them they were wasting their time and trying to start a race war in Mississippi, and if they let me go, I would go back to the train station and sit with the blacks.

They let me go and I went back to the train station. The second time they arrested me they put me in jail. Soon I was in maximum security in Parchman, in a cell next to James Farmer, the head of CORE.

BORN

December 30, 1926, in New York City. Served in the 11th Airborne during World War II, part of the force that occupied Japan after the war.

THEN

English instructor, Oklahoma State University. One of the few Freedom Riders arrested in Jackson who came alone, without working through organizers.

SINCE THEN

Real estate developer in Boulder, CO.

Photographed
September 11, 2005
Boulder, CO
Age: 78

ILLINOIS CENTRAL TRAIN STATION

JUNE 20

New Orleans to Jackson

Rita Carter
21027 Oakland, CA - Age 18

Margaret Kerr
21031 Berkeley, CA - Age 26

Robert Martinson
21037 Berkeley, CA - Age 34

Paul McConnell
21038 Alameda, CA - Age 27

Frederick Muntean
21036 Youngstown, OH - Age 22

Rev. Grant Muse, Jr.
21033 Berkeley, CA - Age 35

Lestra Peterson
21035 Berkeley, CA - Age 23

Joan Pleune
21032 Berkeley, CA - Age 22

Joseph Pratt
21030 San Francisco, CA - Age 19

Jorgia Siegel
21034 Berkeley, CA - Age 19

Buron Teale
21028 Albany, CA - Age 32

Lawrence Triss, Jr.
21040 Berkeley, CA - Age 28 - Died 2001

Thomas Van Roland
21029 Berkeley, CA - Age 24

William Wagoner
21039 Berkeley, CA - Age 30

JOAN PLEUNE

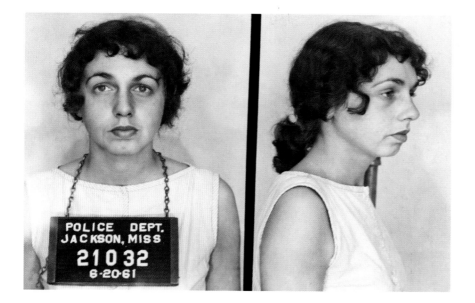

POLICE DEPT.
JACKSON, MISS
21032
6-20-61

BORN

February 17, 1939, in Newark, NJ. Grew up in Livingston and South Orange, NJ.

THEN

Senior at the University of California, Berkeley, where she was an active member of CORE and the Young People's Socialist League. Her younger sister, Alice, had been arrested ten days earlier as a Freedom Rider.

SINCE THEN

Moved to New York City after the Freedom Rides. Since 1985 she has been involved in literacy programs in the city, working with various organizations, including the New York Public Library.

A member of the Granny Peace Brigade since its founding in 2005, she has been active in protests against the Iraq War and has been arrested numerous times.

The Jackson police didn't quite know what to do with me once they arrested me, because I didn't look particularly Caucasian to them. I was pretty tan. I tan easily. They probably thought I was mixed or Creole.

So first they put me in the black cell. There were two cells for women there, one for black women and one for white. And then they realized that this other person [her sister, Alice, had been arrested ten days earlier] and I had the same last name and it wasn't that common a name and she was clearly white. So they moved me to the white cell. It really just showed you how silly it all was.

Photographed
June 7, 2007
New York, NY
Age: 68

JORGIA SIEGEL

I raised money for CORE for about six months after I got to New York City.
I worked at the New York Public Library, and I would go and talk to anybody who would listen to me. I would go and say, "Do you know what's going on here? Well, you need to."

I wore my Freedom Rider button wherever I went, so people would ask me what it was. Then I would ask them, "Are you interested? Would you give me money?" [*Laughs.*]

One day I'm waiting in line to get into the United Nations, and this man comes by, and he says, "You were on the Freedom Rides? What is that?" I told him and then I asked him for money. He says, "No, you come with me." He took me inside the United Nations. He was one of the aides from an African country.

It just seemed like the Freedom Rides would just sort of open all these doors, and all these kinds of things would happen. I gave talks in New York all over the place. People would have a party in their house, and they would invite me. I would tell about my experience, and then they'd pass the hat. I'd get maybe $100, or whatever. I'd give the money to CORE.

BORN
April 21, 1942, in Baltimore, MD, and grew up there.

THEN
Freshman, University of California at Berkeley.

SINCE THEN
Moved to New York City and raised money for CORE, then volunteered with SCLC. Worked on the 1963 March of Washington. Worked briefly at the New York Public Library, then got a nursing degree at Brooklyn College. Moved to Los Angeles in 1966, and then to Santa Barbara in 1971, where she still lives and teaches Lamaze childbirth classes.

Photographed
February 7, 2007
Santa Barbara, CA
Age: 64

TRAILWAYS

JUNE 21

Montgomery to Jackson

Judith Frieze
21047 Northampton, MA - Age 22

Margaret Leonard
21046 New Orleans, LA - Age 19

Samuel Nash
21044 Chicago, IL - Age 24

Mimi Real
21048 Swarthmore, PA - Age 20

Henry Schwarzschild
21041 Highland Park, IL - Age 35 - Died 1996

Rev. Leon Smith, Jr.
21045 Cleveland, OH - Age 32

Theresa Walker
21043 Atlanta, GA - Age 33

Wyatt Tee Walker
21049 Atlanta, GA - Age 31

Melvin White
21042 Talladega, AL - Age 19

LIVINGSTON PARK

JUNE 22

Jackson

Maxie Gardner
21057 Jackson, MS - Age 19

Jimmy Knight
21055 Hattiesburg, MS - Age 21

Elihu Osby, Jr.
21053 Los Angeles, CA - Age 19

Charles Purnell
21054 Jackson, MS - Age 20

TRAILWAYS

JUNE 23

Jackson

Thomas Armstrong III
21060 Jackson, MS - Age 19

Mary Harrison
21058 Jackson, MS - Age 21

Elnora Price
21059 Raymond, MS - Age 26

Joseph Ross
21061 Nashville, TN - Age 25

MIMI REAL

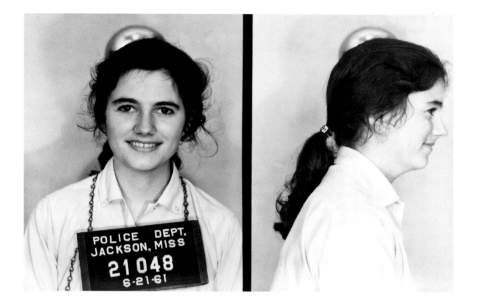

POLICE DEPT.
JACKSON, MISS
21048
6-21-61

BORN

May 31, 1941, in Brooklyn, NY, and grew up there. In high school, organized a busload of fellow students to attend a march in support of school integration, in Washington, DC, in the wake of *Brown* vs. *Board of Education*.

THEN

Sophomore, Swarthmore College, Swarthmore, PA. Active politically, picketing local businesses in support of the student sit-ins in the South in 1960. Volunteered briefly at CORE headquarters in New York City in the summer of 1961 before traveling to Mississippi.

SINCE THEN

After graduating in 1963, worked with CORE in Louisiana on voter registration for over a year. Got a master's degree in American history at the University of Wisconsin, in Madison, over the next two years, returning to the South in the summers to interview civil rights workers and collect documents. Today, the Wisconsin State Historical Society has an extensive archive from the Civil Rights era.

Moved to San Francisco in 1967, and soon became an oral historian, working ten years for the Berkeley Oral History Project, then running her own business, creating oral histories for companies. Today she lives in Marin County and works as an administrator in a private school.

Photographed
February 16, 2007
San Anselmo, CA
Age: 65

At Parchman we had the day very organized because we discovered very early on that if it wasn't, we'd all be talking, and the noise level—it was a cement-block building and the babel would be just unbelievable.

One of the black women was kind of the master of the day, and she would announce what period it was. We had quiet periods and free-talking periods, and then we would have periods where there would be something organized going on.

Somebody would lead exercising— we'd each be doing it in our cells. The cells were very small, but we'd figured out if you'd walked back and forth 1,000 times or something you'd walked a mile.

Then in the evening we had this radio program. It was a variety show. I think the same person was the announcer every night. And each cell had to have something prepared. It could be anything, a Bible reading or a sermon or a talk about something, or you could sing a song, tell a joke, or do a commercial.

One of things we were issued was a bar of soap, which, of course, was absolutely dreadful. It was like lye. So we'd have these commercials about, if you want radiant skin, use Parchman's Soap. We'd have commercials about the skirts, and about the food.

And so we'd go all the way down the cells, and each cell would do its little act, and then the announcer would wrap up, "Well, that's it for Parchman Hour." It was the highlight of our day.

MARGARET LEONARD

My mother was scared for me. So when I was in the Hinds County jail in Jackson, she called them up a lot to see how I was doing. She made it real funny, but she wanted them to know, "We're watching to see how you're treating her."

Everybody called me Sissy. And she would call them and say, "Now Sissy likes scrambled eggs, she doesn't like fried eggs." And the guy said, "We don't have no scrambled eggs here." [*Laughs.*]

But she was hooking in with them: "I know one of those people, I want to be sure you know I know what's happening to her.'"

BORN

January 5, 1942, in Louisville, KY. Grew up in Macon, GA, and Atlanta. Her parents were both newspaper reporters; in the late fifties and early sixties, her mother wrote a column for the *Atlanta Journal* and was known for her "integrationist" views.

THEN

Sophomore, Sophie Newcomb College, in New Orleans; had participated in several CORE demonstrations there.

SINCE THEN

Spent most of her career as a newspaper reporter and editor, working at the *Chattanooga Times,* 1967 to 1973, then at the *St. Petersburg Times,* 1973 to 1976. Later worked at the *Palm Beach Post, Miami Herald,* and *Tallahassee Democrat.*

Today she is retired and lives in Tallahassee.

Photographed
May 3, 2007
Tallahasse, FL
Age: 65

POLICE DEPT.
JACKSON, MISS
21046
6-21-61

THERESA WALKER

- - - - - - - - -

I remember the first night in the Jackson city jail we had cold peas and corn. Mimi [Real] and Sissy [Margaret Leonard] were in the cell next to me. I was in a cell by myself. I remember the mice coming up the bars and running across. When I slept, every once in a while I'd do my feet like this [*shuffles her feet*], to try to keep the mice away. [*Laughs.*]

The county jail was worse. We were all in one cell with an open toilet. Seems like if you wanted a drink of water, the water would run hot. If you wanted to bathe, the water would run cold. They gave us dirty mattresses and we put them on the floor. If you woke up at night you would see the bugs crawling over the other girls. It was terrible.

BORN

February 27, 1928, in Freehold, NJ. Grew up there, in Vauxhall, NJ, and Washington, DC. Attended Virginia Union University in Richmond, VA, then transferred to Howard University, in Washington, DC, where she graduated in 1950. Married Wyatt Tee Walker that same year.

THEN

Living in Atlanta with Wyatt and raising their four children.

SINCE THEN

Was beaten and briefly hospitalized during the Birmingham Campaign in 1963; later arrested, along with her four children, on returning to Atlanta for supposedly evading arrest. Arrested in New York City in 2000 during protests over the police killing of Amadou Diallo. Now lives with Wyatt outside Richmond, VA.

Photographed
July 11, 2006
Chester, VA
Age: 78

WYATT TEE WALKER

My father was a preacher and was what we called in the black community a race man. I got my feeling of anti-segregation from him, just passed down. My father told me many times about how he'd gone into the Emporia, VA, train station and it was cold, and he was in the white waiting room, the only waiting room, and the constable came in there and raised his stick. My father said he had a .32 pistol, Smith & Wesson, nickel-plated. He said that if the constable started down with that club, he was going to shoot him. So that was always my point of reference.

When I first came to Petersburg [VA] as a pastor, I used to carry a gun. I was waiting for some racist to have a confrontation with me so I'd have an excuse to shoot him. And then, of course, I met Martin Luther King. I came under his influence and he made me put up my gun.

BORN

August 16, 1929, in Brockton, MA. Grew up in Merchantville, NJ.

THEN

Executive director, Southern Christian Leadership Conference, Martin Luther King's organization. A graduate of Virginia Union University in Richmond in 1950, and from the university's seminary in 1953. Had married Theresa Walker in 1950. Became pastor of the Gillfield Baptist Church in Petersburg, VA, and served as head of the NAACP chapter in Petersburg and the state director of CORE. In 1958 he joined the board of the SCLC and in 1960 moved to Atlanta to become its executive director.

SINCE THEN

Ran the SCLC until 1964. From 1967 until he retired in 2004 he was the pastor at the Canaan Baptist Church of Christ in Harlem. He and Theresa now live outside Richmond, VA.

Photographed
July 11, 2006
Chester, VA
Age: 76

CHARLES PURNELL

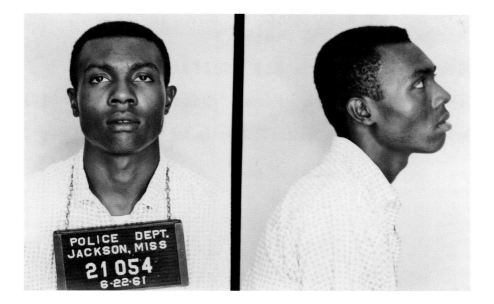

POLICE DEPT.
JACKSON, MISS
21 054
6-22-61

BORN
January 19, 1941, in Rolling Fork, MS. Grew up there and in several other small towns in the Delta and north Mississippi, including Cleveland, Coldwater, and Holly Bluff, and in Alto, LA. His father was an African Methodist Episcopal preacher who liked to change churches every two years.

THEN
Student, Campbell Junior College, in Jackson.

SINCE THEN
Graduated Campbell and entered Tougaloo College, in Jackson. Enlisted in the Army and served three years, including a twelve-month tour in South Korea, 1964–65. Graduated from Tougaloo College in 1969. Graduated from Turner Theological Seminary, in Atlanta, in 1976.

Has been the pastor of the Bethel AME church in Savannah, GA, since 1990. Before that he led other AME churches in Savannah, Columbus, and Atlanta.

Photographed
May 5, 2007
Savannah, GA
Age: 66

I was in high school in Cleveland, MS, when we got word about the murder of Emmett Till. [Cleveland is about thirty-five miles from Money, where Till was abducted and later murdered.]

I had heard growing up that you weren't supposed to look at a white woman eye-to-eye, nor a white person. You were expected to look down, and I don't recall ever doing that. What I developed very early in life, I was just as important as they were, and I had no need to look. If my attention was not called, I had no need to look in that direction. I only asked for what I needed in stores or whatever, and purchased that, and went forth. I never spent any time on street corners, as was a custom of young persons who were not disciplined by their parents. My daddy was a very strict disciplinarian and a preacher, so we did not get an opportunity to even be enticed.

Dad often spoke from the pulpit about the dignity of black people. He had a work ethic that he felt that we should embrace. And he always said that nobody was going to come in his home, as long as he had breath, to do any harm. He perhaps inherited this last from my granddaddy, who died before I was born.

He was a farmer and was an expert Winchester shooter, so he developed a reputation as being a crazy black person. Apparently there was a little bit of anger when he was stirred up. My father was also easily stirred up. As long as Daddy got along with white folk, he was okay. He would always correct them for referring to him as "boy" or "uncle." I remember on several occasions in my presence he did that.

THOMAS ARMSTRONG III

I've always felt that many people who participated and were deeply committed to the movement became wounded. I read somewhere where someone used the phrase "walking wounded" to describe us. I believe that. I look around at friends of mine and people that I knew who were in the movement. I think it did affect them in certain respects. And there was nothing in the black communities to help these people deal with that. To help those people overcome that depression. They call it post-traumatic syndrome. They received no help.

I think that's what part of my problem was at that time. I started to get depressed, and I think one of the reasons for the depression I felt was that I couldn't go back and participate more.

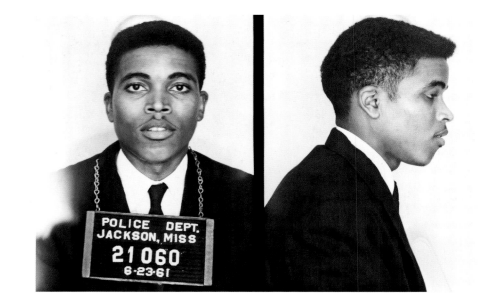

BORN
August 17, 1941, in Silver Creek, MS, and grew up there.

THEN
Sophomore at Tougaloo College in Jackson. Active with the NAACP in Jackson on voter registration and other projects.

SINCE THEN
Continued to work in the movement in Mississippi, doing voter registration work and trying to integrate white churches on Sundays. Left Mississippi briefly to live in Kansas City, then returned. Attempted to integrate Millsaps in 1964, a private Methodist college in Jackson, but the class he registered for was canceled.

Moved to Chicago and in 1966 began working as a contract specialist with the U.S. Postal Service, managing trucking services. Now retired and lives in Naperville, IL.

Photographed
September 16, 2005
Naperville, IL
Age: 64

ILLINOIS CENTRAL TRAIN STATION

JUNE 25

New Orleans to Jackson

George Blevins
21065 Los Angeles, CA - Age 21

Gloria Bouknight
21070 Columbia, SC - Age 20

Arthur Brooks, Jr.
21066 Los Angeles, CA - Age 22

John Dolan
21080 Berkeley, CA - Age 20

Mary Hamilton
21068 Los Angeles, CA - Age 25

Gordon Harris
21078 Rochester, NY - Age 23

Louise Inghram
21074 Los Angeles, CA - Age 26

Frank Johnson
21076 Tucson, AZ - Age 21 - Died 1997

Marian Kendall
21064 Philadelphia, PA - Age 35 – Died 2002

Claude Liggins
21075 Los Angeles, CA - Age 20

Chela Lightchild
21067 Los Angeles, CA - Age 23

Norma Libson
21082 New Orleans, TN - Age 27

Eddora Manning
21083 Los Angeles, CA - Age 19

Robert Mason
21072 Los Angeles, CA - Age 17

Frank Nelson
21079 Brooklyn, NY - Age 22 - Died 2005

Janis Rogers
21069 Los Angeles, CA - Age 25

John Rogers
21071 Los Angeles, CA - Age 30 - Died 1994

Wayne Taylor
21077 Los Angeles, CA - Age 23

Claire Toombs
21081 Silver Springs, MD - Age 18

JOHN DOLAN

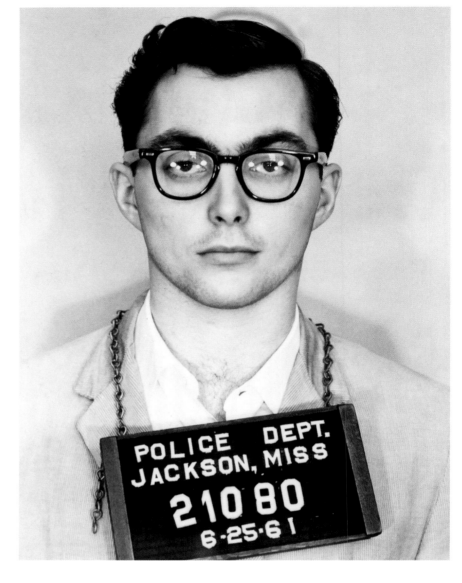

- - - - - - - - -

In Parchman we had very few ways of getting our point across.

The only thing we could do is refuse to hand back our food trays. Frank [Nelson] and I were real tough. We were the hardest. We refused to hand the trays back, so they threw us in the hole, which literally was a hole. It was dark; they didn't feed us; it just had running water and a little hole where you urinate and defecate. We were three days there.

Frank and I were in jail about six weeks total, about a week of it in solitary. I was kind of proud, and I lost a lot of weight. We stayed the first night in New Orleans, at the YMCA, and I went down to lift weights. I saw these guys picking up eighty-five pounds, which I thought was practically nothing. I went over to pick it up, and I almost fell over. I couldn't believe it. I'd lost all my strength.

BORN
April 11, 1941, in San Francisco. Grew up in San Mateo and elsewhere in the Bay Area.

THEN
Junior at the University of California, Berkeley; active member of the local CORE chapter.

SINCE THEN
Worked briefly with CORE in New Orleans before returning to the West Coast. Graduated Berkeley in 1962, and medical school at UC-San Francisco in 1968. Specialized in emergency medicine, and practiced in the Bay Area full-time until 1998. Today he practices part-time at the VA clinic in Oakland.

Photographed
September 5, 2005
Emeryville, CA
Age: 64

GORDON HARRIS

One of the guards at the county jail kept coming up to our cell — this is a white guy — I don't know out of guilt or what, but I can remember the phrase. "We don't hate our niggers," he said. "You don't understand us. We don't hate our niggers."

BORN
February 24, 1938, in Charleston, SC. Grew up in Rochester, NY. A member of a NAACP youth group in junior high and high school.

THEN
Student at the University of Rochester, where he had helped start a CORE chapter. Also a conscientious objector.

SINCE THEN
Came back to the South in 1962, doing voter registration work in several places, including Chattanooga, TN, and Clarksdale, MS. Arrested during a march in Gadsen, AL, and spent a month in jail there. Graduated from Wilmington College, in Wilmington, OH, in 1967, then worked in Cleveland as an investigator for the Ohio Civil Rights Commission, then for the American Friends Service Committee.

Graduated Earlham School of Religion, a Quaker seminary in Richmond, IN, in 1974. Led a church in Central City, NE, for four years. Later moved to Winthrop, ME, and had a church there. Now lives in Lewiston, ME, where has been involved in efforts to support the African emigrant community there. He has a therapy dog, a daschund named Scotty, whom he takes to retirement homes to visit with the residents once a week.

Photographed
June 21, 2007
Lewiston, ME
Age: 69

CLAUDE LIGGINS

I'm so glad I took the trip, became involved, because every now and then I meet somebody and we'll be out in public and they remember my name. They say, "Claude Liggins, you really did a fantastic job. You helped change the city." It's a good feeling to look back at something historical that you were a part of.

I remember I was in high school when I first read about the Boston Tea Party, and I used to imagine myself being in that kind of thing, wanting to know how it felt to be part of some historical thing. Now I can say I have been a part of something historical. It's a good feeling, because there are a lot of people who have done a lot of things, got rich, got poor, but whatever they have accomplished, they can't touch what I did. Not even Oprah can do that, and she got a lot of money.

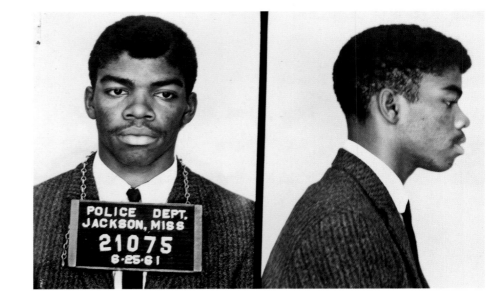

BORN
December 3, 1940, in Lake Charles, LA, and grew up there.

THEN
Student, City College, Los Angeles. Had been living in Los Angeles since 1959.

SINCE THEN
Very active in the civil rights movement in Los Angeles in the early 1960s, working with CORE and SNCC; arrested many times. Ran his own graphic design business, retiring in 2007.

Photographed
February 8, 2007
Los Angeles, CA
Age: 66

CHELA LIGHTCHILD

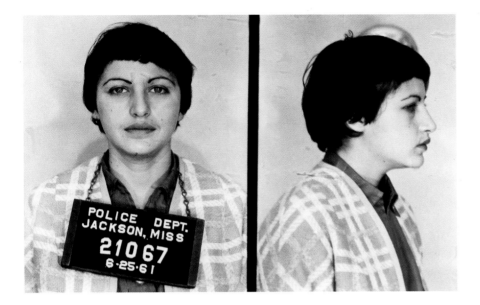

POLICE DEPT.
JACKSON, MISS
21067
6·25·61

BORN
Marcia Rosenbaum on May 23, 1938, in Newark, NJ. Grew up there and in Sacramento, CA.

THEN
In Los Angeles since 1959, working for the Fellowship of Reconciliation and studying Gandhi and nonviolence. Briefly attended UCLA when she first moved there.

SINCE THEN
Worked for CORE, first in New Orleans, from the fall of 1961 to 1963, then in Los Angeles. Arrested several times in both cities. Also active in the anti-war movement. In 1967, she and her husband moved back to the land, living in Oregon and northern California for four years.

In 1971, she and her husband joined the Peace Corps, and worked for two years in the Dominican Republic, promoting organic farming. In 1972 she changed her name to Chela Lightchild.

Taught agriculture with her husband at Emerson College, in Sussex, England, for four years, then returned to the Dominican Republic, where they continued to promote organic farming.

Retired in 1988 and moved with her husband to Las Vegas, NM.

Capt. [J. L.] Ray called out our names and put us under arrest. When he called Mary Hamilton's name and she stepped forward, they said, "No, you're white. You can't be Mary Hamilton."

They pulled me out and said, "You're Mary Hamilton." Because I was tan, dark—I spent a lot of time at the beach—and Mary Hamilton was very light colored.

I tried to explain, Mary and I both tried. They were mad at us. They said, "Don't try to mess with us. We can see who's white and who's black."

I thought it was funny. The *LA Times* had a picture of me laughing hysterically because they were pushing me in the police car with all these black people. We thought that was really funny. They couldn't tell white from black.

So they put me in the car with the black people and took me to the jail and sat me in with the blacks and Mary with the whites and then later when the fingerprints came back they found out they had made a mistake. They didn't like that. So I got a little roughed up and I guess Mary got a little roughed up, because we'd integrated the cells.

Photographed
May 21, 2007
Las Vegas, NM
Age: 68

TRAILWAYS

JULY 2

Montgomery to Jackson

Barbara Kay
21095 Englewood, NJ - Age 35 - Died 1997

Robert Miller
21097 Detroit, MI - Age 22

Michael Pritchard
21098 San Francisco, CA - Age 18

Peter Stoner
21099 Chicago, IL - Age 22

Leotis Thornton
21096 San Jose, CA - Age 23 - Died 1976

LIVINGSTON PARK

JULY 5*

Jackson

Mary Lou Bell
21107 Jackson, MS - Age 18

Charles Brice
21108 Jackson, MS - Age 19

Eddie Thomas
21106 Jackson, MS - Age 20

Percy Thornton
21105 Jackson, MS - Age 18

TRAILWAYS

JULY 5*

Jackson

Robert Bass
21104 Jackson, MS - Age 18

Ralph Floyd
21103 Jackson, MS - Age 18

Eugene Lee
21102 Raymond, MS - Age 26

* Although the dates in the mug shots say July 4, all other documents indicate that the arrests came a day later, on July 5.

PETER STONER

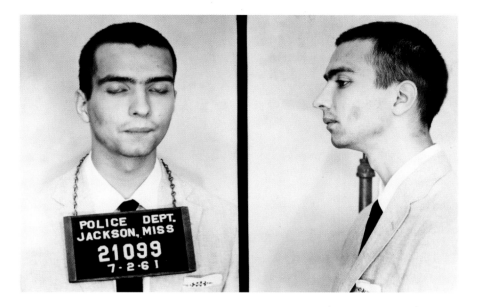

BORN

December 28, 1938, in Milton, MA. Grew up Berlin, PA.

THEN

Student at the University of Chicago, where he enrolled without
having finished high school.

SINCE THEN

Transferred to Tougaloo College, in Jackson, where he later graduated.
Worked throughout Mississippi in the civil rights movement during the
sixties and was frequently arrested. Later got a master's degree and
Ph.D. in chemistry at the University of Southern Mississippi, in
Hattiesburg. Returned to Jackson, where he has worked as a car
mechanic, for others and for himself.

**At Parchman I was housed
in a large room with maybe
forty to fifty white men.**
Most of the men were young college
students like myself. We weren't
allowed any reading material; the
room was furnished with beds only.
Mostly, we just sat around and talked.
One of the men there had been
somewhat of an alcoholic. I had
known him previously in Chicago—
and was having a hard time. He
commented one time that the jailers
weren't any different now than they
were at the time of Christ. I
remember asking him if the drunks
were any different nowadays.

Photographed
April 22, 2007
Jackson, MS
Age: 68

TRAILWAYS

JULY 5

Jackson

Marshall Bennett
21110 Jackson, MS - Age 18

Miller G. Green
21109 Jackson, MS - Age 18

Robert Green
21111 Jackson, MS - Age 18

Jesse Harris
21114 Jackson, MS - Age 18

Percy Johnson
21113 Jackson, MS - Age 18

James Jones
21112 Jackson, MS - Age 18

ILLINOIS CENTRAL TRAIN STATION

JULY 6

Jackson

Frank Caston
21119 Jackson, MS - Age 18

Frank Griffin
21117 Jackson, MS - Age 21

Alpha Palmer
21116 Jackson, MS - Age 19 - Died 2003

West Phillips
21120 Jackson, MS - Age 19

Tommie Watts, Jr.
21118 Jackson, MS - Age 17

Mack Wells
18023 Jackson, MS - Age 20

MILLER G. GREEN

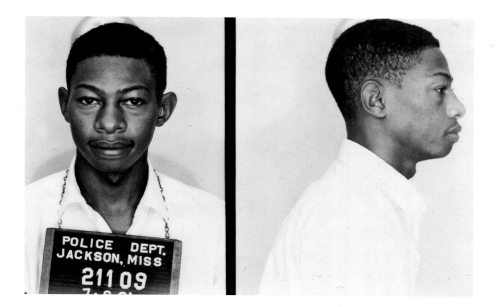

BORN

May 19, 1943, in Bentonia, MS. Grew up in Jackson.

THEN

Senior, Lanier High School.

SINCE THEN

Worked in the civil rights movement in Mississippi doing voter registration. Attended Utica Junior College, in nearby Utica, for a year.

Moved to Chicago in 1963. Worked in a printing plant and a prepared foods factory; active in the movement, working with Operation Breadbasket and Operation PUSH to improve economic opportunities in black communities.

In the mid-seventies and early eighties started and ran several businesses, including clothing stores and a hair salon. Later worked as a director of security for St. Bernard Hospital, and as a manager of a blood bank. Today he lives in the Englewood neighborhood in Chicago and runs Citizens for a Better West Englewood.

What happened in Mississippi was basically the whole state was put on a bunch of young people, seventeen, eighteen years old.

The ministers ran. They went fishing. The Ph.D.s, they ran. So it came down to a bunch of teenagers who grew up in Mississippi and knew the situation, who knew what the consequences could be. Yet we carried that on our shoulders. The adults was nowhere to be found.

The only somebody I know that was an adult at the time was Medgar Evers [the NAACP field secretary in Mississippi]. Everybody else disappeared. Nobody was there. It was a very frustrating situation, to know that there were no adults who was willing to take that chance.

We had seen what had been done to Emmett Till. I remember when it happened. The fear escalated so that when it got dark and you was away from home and you saw car lights coming on, you ran, not knowing who would be in that car. We lived with that. And come 1961, you asking young men to go and do something that they'd seen nobody ever do.

Photographed
November 22, 2006
Chicago, IL
Age: 63

JESSE HARRIS

James Bevel came to the place where we hung out at—it was like a pool hall.
He said, "Hey, we got this bus coming in. People are gonna be protesting at the Trailways bus station and they need local support."

That's where my education started. People had to be oriented in the philosophy of nonviolence, which was a new thing to me. Because we were gang members, now. You might say that I was one of the leaders of the Georgetown Gang.

When I got out of jail, everybody said, "Hey!" And I said, "Well, you gotta go, too. You ain't nothing until you go to jail. You Uncle Tom till you go to jail."

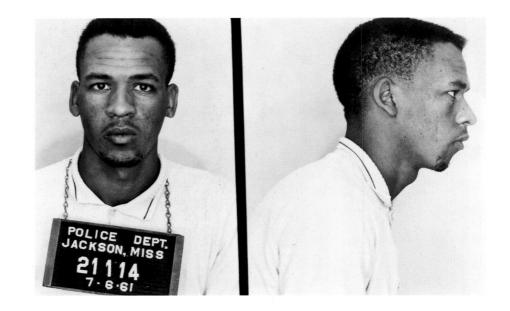

BORN
January 10, 1940, in Jackson, and grew up there.

THEN
Student, Lanier High School.

SINCE THEN
In the early sixties worked on voter registration campaigns around Mississippi, especially in the Delta. In 1964 helped train Freedom Summer volunteers before they came to Mississippi, and managed the volunteers in and around McComb. Also organized for the Mississippi Freedom Democratic Party. In the mid-sixties worked for the Child Development Group of Mississippi, a predecessor to Head Start. Later worked with the Poor People's Corporation and the Federation of Southern Coops, which were trying to improve the economic opportunities for black craftspeople and farmers.

In the late sixties and early seventies was a member of Nation of Islam, and lived briefly in Chicago and New York. Later moved to Florida where he lived for ten years in Ft. Lauderdale and twenty-five in Miami, working in various jobs, including as a longshoreman, a truck driver, an airplane engine mechanic, and an instructor for a community college golf team. Now retired and lives in Jackson. Each summer participates in a program at a nearby public golf course, teaching children how to play.

Photographed
April 3, 2007
Jackson, MS
Age: 67

FRANK GRIFFIN

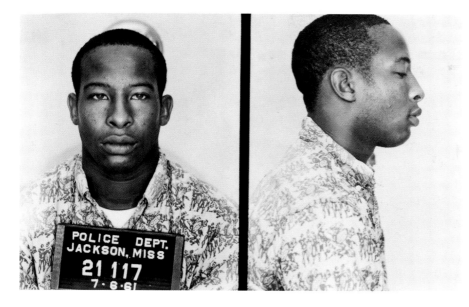

POLICE DEPT.
JACKSON, MISS
21 117
7·6·61

BORN
July 9, 1940, in Lena, MS. Grew up in Carthage and Jackson.

THEN
Student at Alabama State, in Montgomery.

SINCE THEN
After graduating from Alabama State, moved to Demopolis, AL, where his wife is from. Taught history and coached basketball in the public schools there for ten years, then worked in a cement plant for twenty-six years.

Now retired, still lives in Demopolis with his wife.

I was brought up on a farm. Cotton, corn, stuff like that. Granddaddy was a farmer. It was constant work. If you weren't picking cotton you were plowing. If you weren't plowing you was cutting the fence lines. When we weren't working in our fields, we was working in the white man's fields.

On Saturday we rode on the wagon to the one general store in downtown Carthage. They had one movie theater on the square, and then a general store around the square on the corner. We got what we needed for the house, maybe a pair of shoes or a pair of pants or a shirt. That was about it.

It was very intimidating and very scary. We weren't allowed in the front. We tied the wagon in the back, got what we wanted, and carried it out the back. We mostly stayed behind Granddaddy and he took care of all the business.

We usually had problems going back home. They'd yell at us to get out of the way. Made us get off the road. They'd holler out the N-word. Granddaddy would just pull over and let them pass and then we'd start off again. Maybe we'd have to do that two or three times on the way home.

Sometimes at night they'd come back and throw rocks and bricks on the porch and stuff like that. Holler that N-word at us and Granddad would get us all in one big room and finally they'd go home. They never would try to come in.

Photographed
April 29, 2007
Demopolis, AL
Age: 66

147

GREYHOUND

JULY 7

Jackson

Alfonzo Denson, Jr.
21128 Jackson, MS - Age 18

Samuel Givens
21131 Jackson, MS - Age 16

Landy McNair, Jr.
21124 Jackson, MS - Age 18

Earl Vance, Jr.
21123 Jackson, MS - Age 19 - Died 1974

Hezekiah Watkins
21129 Jackson, MS - Age 13

Paul Young
21130 Jackson, MS - Age 16

TRAILWAYS

JULY 7

Montgomery to Jackson

Charles Biggers
21137 Boulder, CO - Age 23

Elmer Brown
21139 Akron, OH - Age 20

William Hansen, Jr.
21135 Cincinnati, OH - Age 21

John Lowry
21133 New York, NY - Age 20

Norma Matzkin
21134 New York, NY - Age 27

Isaac Reynolds, Jr.
21138 Detroit, MI - Age 27 - Died 1998

Daniel Stevens
21132 Wilmington, OH - Age 19

Ameen Tuungane
21136 Columbus, OH - Age 20

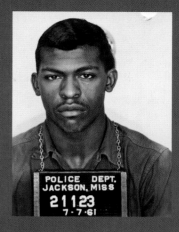

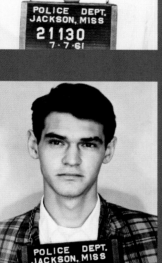

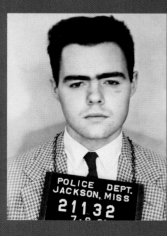

HEZEKIAH WATKINS

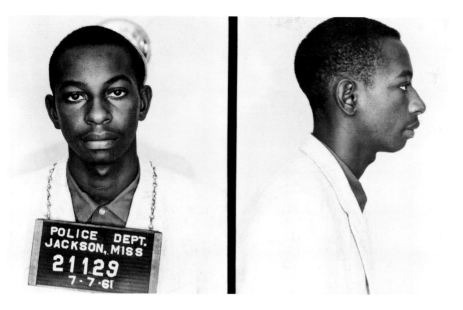

POLICE DEPT.
JACKSON, MISS
21129
7-7-61

BORN

September 1, 1947, in Milwaukee, WI. Grew up on a farm in Rankin County, east of Jackson, MS, and in Jackson.

THEN

Ninth-grade student, Rowan Junior High, in Jackson.

SINCE THEN

Active in the movement during his high school years at Lanier, where he graduated in 1965. Attended Utica Junior College in nearby Utica. Drafted into the army in 1967 and served two years, including a tour in South Korea, along the DMZ.

Returned to Jackson and worked for the Jackson-Hinds Comprehensive Health Agency, then the Hinds County Human Resource Agency. In 1987, bought a small grocery near the Jackson State University campus, which he still runs today. Remains active in local community affairs.

Photographed
April 21, 2007
Jackson, MS
Age: 59

Growing up in Jackson, the only time we would encounter something is when we went downtown. That was on Capitol, the major street in Jackson. That's when the names began to ring out. That's when if a white person was approaching you, you almost had to get in the street to let them by. That's when it really dawned on me about the black/white situation.

There were several water fountains on Capitol Street. The signs read, "White only, colored only," and I really didn't know what colored was in terms of drinking. I think it was my mom informed me that, "If you get thirsty while you're downtown, make sure you drink from this side of the fountain," which read, "Colored." I said, "Yes, ma'am, okay."

The older I got, the more racial prejudice I encountered with whites, especially at night. I started working as a dishwasher. I was so small and so short they had to stack Coca-Cola cases for me to stand on to put the dishes in the rack to run 'em through the dishwasher. A few nights when I got off work I would walk home.

During that time, we would encounter white police officers and white teenagers who would basically run us home, run us between houses. They ran us under houses. We never was beaten. They would shoot their guns. But I'm sure now—I wasn't aware of it then—the guns was fired in the air, because if they wanted to shoot us, injure us, or kill us, they had an opportunity to do so.

DANIEL STEVENS

In the first offenders camp at Parchman, I found myself bedded down next to an unusual Freedom Rider. I think his name was Morty.

He was not through CORE. He was a little Brooklyn guy who decided on his own to come down and join the Freedom Rides but he didn't quite know how. So he came to Jackson, got a library card, took out an awful lot of library books, and shipped them back to his home in Brooklyn because he thought Jackson should be punished. Then he just hung around the bus station until our group showed up, and he came and sat with us and got arrested.

Photographed
November 14, 2006
Hyde Park, IL
Age: 64

BORN
May 4, 1942, in Wauseon, OH, and grew up on a farm nearby. At fifteen, moved with his mother and brothers to a Bruderhof intentional community in upstate New York. After eighteen months there they moved to Saginaw, MI.

THEN
Freshman at Wilmington College, in Wilmington, OH; active in the CORE chapter there.

SINCE THEN
Worked for several months with sharecroppers in western Tennessee who were trying to register to vote. Moved to New York City, and was active in civil rights efforts and, later, anti-war demonstrations there. Moved to San Francisco in 1968 and with his partner started a candle-making business. Moved to Martinsburg, WV, with his partner, and continued to make candles.

Returned to college in 1980, first at Shephard College, in Shephardstown, WV, then at the University of Chicago. Worked as a computer programmer for the university from 1988 to 1996, then as a consultant, mostly for clients in New York and Seattle. Now retired and lives in Hyde Park, IL.

AMEEN TUUNGANE

BORN

Willie James Thomas on July 21, 1940, in Cincinnati, OH, and grew up there.

THEN

Junior, Ohio University, in Athens. Had participated in several civil rights demonstrations in Cincinnati and worked on membership drives for the local chapter of NAACP.

SINCE THEN

Continued his studies at Ohio University, alternating with work. Graduated in 1979 from the University of Cincinatti with a degree in electrical engineering and moved to Birmingham, AL. Worked for a regional utility company from 1980 to 1988. Since then has worked as a financial consultant. Converted to Islam in 1995 and changed his name.

Photographed
April 27, 2007
Bessemer, AL
Age: 66

There was a transition between NAACP and CORE. The local NAACP [in Cincinatti] had a lot of top lawyers. Pretty much every black lawyer at the time was an NAACP lawyer. You couldn't be a lawyer and not be in NAACP, so all the lawyers were there.

But it wasn't anything the youth could get involved with. Meanwhile, we saw the dynamics were such that if a man who worked at XYZ factory or worked at XYZ school and his wife tried to do something, he could be fired. But a kid who's not working cannot be threatened with losing his job. [*Laughs.*]

The only thing they could threaten us with was, we lose X amount of years in getting a college degree. I saw it, and a lot of the other students saw it, as, "You can't hurt us like you can hurt them, so we're coming." So I joined that wave. Right around then, that's when CORE started the Freedom Ride.

I knew about CORE. A lot of the younger people started seeing that NAACP wasn't moving fast enough for us. We saw CORE as more of a direct action thing we could do, and we saw how it could work.

There was the group that got beat up in Anniston real bad. I knew one closely. They went on into Mississippi and there was like a wave that went in and then it slowed down. [Mississippi governor] Ross Barnett came on the air and said he was teaching us a lesson and we were scared to come. I was part of the next wave to come in and say, you know, "There's more of us coming."

ILLINOIS CENTRAL TRAIN STATION

JULY 7

Jackson

Morton Slater

21140 New York, NY - Age 18

ILLINOIS CENTRAL TRAIN STATION

JULY 9

New Orleans to Jackson

Patricia Baskerville

21148 Tucson, AZ - Age 18

Larry Bell

21145 Los Angeles, CA - Age 19

Tommie Brashear

21141 Los Angeles, CA - Age 19

Edmond Dalbert, Jr.

21147 Los Angeles, CA - Age 25

Reginald Jackson

21143 Los Angeles, CA - Age 21 - Died 2000

Edward Johnson

21146 Los Angeles, CA - Age 19

Philip Perkins

21142 Delaware, OH - Age 20

Roena Rand

21149 Los Angeles, CA - Age 29

John Taylor, Jr.

21144 Berkeley, CA - Age 26

LARRY BELL

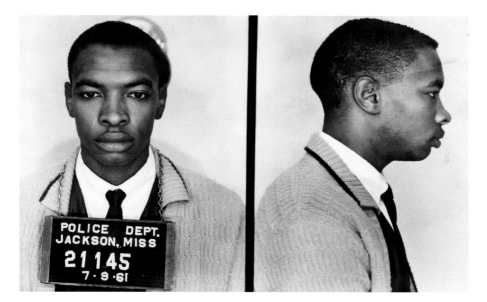

BORN

March 5, 1942, in Monroe, GA. Grew up there and in Los Angeles, where his family moved in 1950.

THEN

Freshman, Los Angeles City College.

SINCE THEN

Returned to Los Angeles, working as a janitor during the day and attending City College at night. In 1966 was one of the first blacks to go to work for United Airlines in California. When he retired in 2000, he was a flight-attendant supervisor and also trained newly hired flight attendants. Still lives in Los Angeles.

The clothing that they gave us in Parchman was a t-shirt that was military green and some green boxer shorts. No shoes, no. And as we began to protest, they took them from us and left us with nothing. Then they took the mattress, so now we had to lie on a metal slab with them little round holes—and boy, you talk about some hard sleeping at night? When you're sleeping on the thing, there's that indentation where your skin goes through that little round hole, and there you are, half of you is like being suffocated and the other half is being cut out, you couldn't sleep any way you tried. So we sat up and we debated all night, and we got more boisterous in our songs.

Photographed
February 9, 2007
Los Angeles, CA
Age: 64

EDWARD JOHNSON

At Parchman they brought some kids in to sight-see us. Elementary school students, white kids. They brought them in and told them to walk close to the wall, away from us. We had just gotten there. The kids wanted to see the Freedom Riders so they brought them in.

They were pointing at us just like we were animals. "Oh, look at that one's hair." "Oh, look at that one."

I guess somebody knew somebody and they brought the kids in to see the Freedom Riders. They were there just a few minutes. They walked down to the end and walked back out, making comments as they went. I put that on me and kept on stepping.

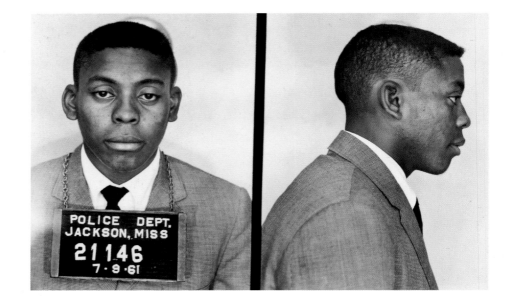

BORN
October 4, 1941, in Houston, TX, and grew up there. Attended University of Texas, in Austin, for a year, then moved to Los Angeles in 1960.

THEN
Living in Los Angeles; had recently quit a job with the post office.

SINCE THEN
Returned to Los Angeles, and alternated working with college. Went to work for Rockwell International in 1972. Graduated from Pepperdine University in 1974. Continued at Rockwell, working primarily on factory automation and robotics. In 1978 went to work at Northrop, focused on data processing and web systems for military projects. Retired in 2006.

Photographed
February 10, 2007
Marina del Rey, CA
Age: 65

TRAILWAYS

JULY 9

Montgomery to Jackson

Daniel Burkholder
21156 Chicago, IL - Age 29

Lionell Goldbart
21152 Brooklyn, NY - Age 27 - Died 2007

Albert Gordon
21150 New York, NY - Age 27

Stephen Greenstein
21155 Brooklyn, NY - Age 22

Jeanne Herrick
21154 Chicago, IL - Age 28

Saul Manfield
21151 Chicago, IL - Age 34 - Died 2005

Robert Rogers
21157 New York, NY - Age 32

Lula White
21153 Chicago, IL - Age 22

TRAILWAYS

JULY 9

Jackson

Leo Blue
21167 Jackson, MS - Age 14 - Died 1988

Mildred Blue
21159 Jackson, MS - Age 16 - Died 1993

Fred Clark
21163 Jackson, MS - Age 18

Jessie Davis
21162 Jackson, MS - Age 19

Gainnel Hayes
21161 Jackson, MS - Age 15

Andrew Horne, Jr.
21166 Jackson, MS - Age 15

Erma Lee Horne
21160 Jackson, MS - Age 16

Delores Lynch
21158 Jackson, MS - Age 15

Vance O'Neal
20324 Jackson, MS - Age 17

Henry Rosell
21164 Jackson, MS - Age 18

Joe Watts, Jr.
21165 Jackson, MS - Age 18 - Died 2003

ALBERT GORDON

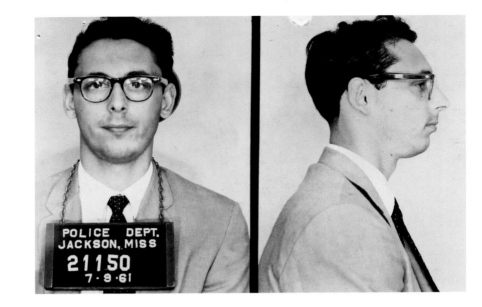

During the thirty-nine days I was in prison we had great conversations, great arguments.
As a historian, I decided to do something historical, and I interviewed people. I took my pad— or maybe I—who remembers? We had pencils at that time. And I interviewed everybody. I asked them their political affiliation and motivation. It was fascinating. The one thing I regret more than anything is that I've never been able to find the results of that.

I do remember I was amazed that there was a big minority of Communists. That really blew my mind, 'cause I had never really known any Communists. There was also an equal minority of religious people— and then everything in between. Many people were highly educated. We had great discussions and arguments. We all learned a lot.

BORN

June 18, 1934, in Antwerp, Belgium. Escaped through France and Spain with his family in late 1941, resettling in Forest Hills in Queens, NY. Graduated from City College in New York in 1955. Drafted into the Navy in 1956 and served nineteen months. Studied for a year at the University of Paris, then got a master's degree in history at Columbia University.

THEN

History teacher at Tilden High School in Brooklyn, NY.

SINCE THEN

Continued to teach in New York City high schools. Became active with the Brooklyn CORE chapter. Returned to Mississippi during Freedom Summer, in 1964, working in the Delta with Fannie Lou Hamer, among many others. Also active in anti-war efforts.

From 1969–85 was a dealer in African art and had a gallery in Manhattan. Served as a Peace Corps volunteer to Niger in 1990–91. Opened a new gallery of African art, Origins, in Stockbridge, MA, in 1996. In 1997 donated a large portion of his personal collection of African art to Tougaloo College in Jackson.

Photographed
June 24, 2007
Stephentown, NY
Age: 73

WALGREEN'S

JULY 11

Luvaghn Brown
21170 Jackson, MS - Age 16

Jimmie Travis
21169 Jackson, MS - Age 18

WALGREEN'S

JULY 13

Jackson

Eddie Austin
20666 Jackson, MS - Age 18

Charles Cox
21177 Jackson, MS - Age 18

William Baker
21178 Port Gibson, MS - Age 19

Carl Hamilton
21176 Jackson, MS - Age 19

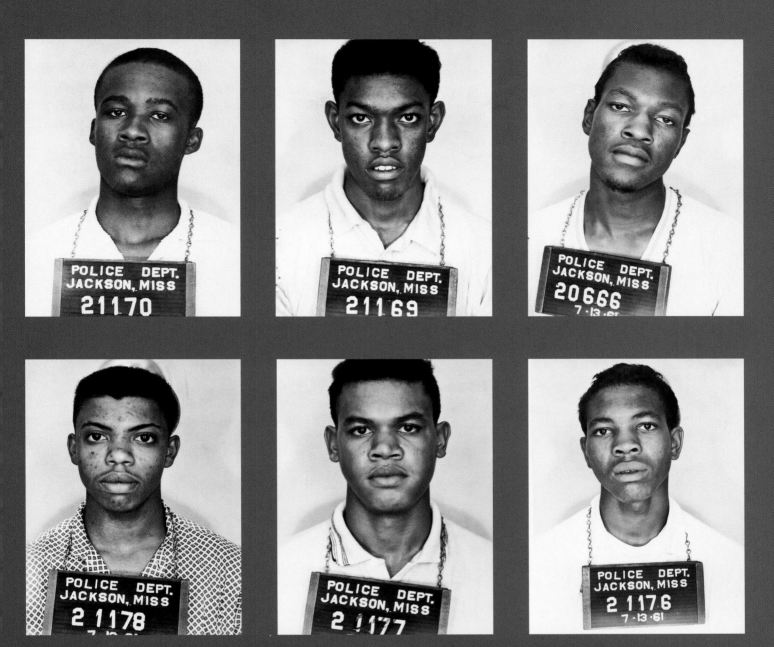

GREYHOUND

JULY 15

New Orleans to Jackson

Carroll Barber
21188 Los Angeles, CA - Age 36 - Died 1999

Charles Booth
21190 Los Angeles, CA - Age 18

Ray Cooper
21189 Spokane, WA - Age 19

Marilyn Eisenberg
21187 Van Nuys, CA - Age 18

Robert Owens
21180 Los Angeles, CA - Age 23

Jean Pestana
21186 Los Angeles, CA - Age 43 - Died 1997

David Richards
21179 Reseda, CA - Age 22 - Died 2000

Rose Rosenberg
21183 Los Angeles, CA - Age 55

Leon Russ, Jr.
21185 Los Angeles, CA - Age 23

Leo Washington
21181 New Orleans, LA - Age 24

Rev. Douglas Williams
21184 Los Angeles, CA - Age 38 - Died 1979

Jack Wolfson
21182 Los Angeles, CA - Age 17

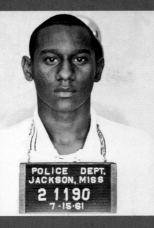

GREYHOUND

JULY 16

Nashville to Jackson

James Dennis
21198 Los Angeles, CA - Age 25

Mary Freelon
21196 Telford, PA - Age 42 - Died 1982

Philip Havey
21194 Staten Island, NY - Age 31

Rudolph Mitaritonna
21191 Bronx, NY - Age 50 - Died 1980

Shirley Smith
21195 New York, NY - Age 34 - Died 2000

Bill Svanoe
21193 New York, NY - Age 23

James Warren
21197 Philadelphia, PA - Age 28

Lewis Zuchman
21192 Bridgeport, CT - Age 19

HEIDELBERG HOTEL

JULY 19

Jackson

Richard Haley
21209 Chicago, IL - Age 45 - Died 1988

Helen O'Neal McCray
21208 Jackson, MS - Age 20

PHILIP HAVEY

I didn't play any chess in the first offenders camp in Parchman. Others were playing it without the pieces, just a board scratched out on the cement. I could follow it a few moves but I wasn't really that much into chess. It really whacked out the guards because they thought maybe somebody could fake it for a little while but these guys would be sitting there at this board and playing it for a long time. The guards were always taking the pieces away. So the real chess people figured to hell with the pieces.

Photographed
February 13, 2007
Albany, CA
Age: 76

BORN

June 29, 1930, in New Rochelle, NY, and grew up there.

In 1949 joined the army and served for a year; later served in the air force from 1951–53, stationed primarily in Okinawa and Nebraska. After being discharged, alternated between college at Iona, in New Rochelle, and working on the construction of the New York State Thruway.

THEN

Living in Manhattan, involved with the Catholic Worker Movement, and active in civil disobedience protests.

SINCE THEN

Continued to be involved with the Catholic Worker Movement, and also worked on major construction projects, including the Verrazano Narrows Bridge, the GM building, and the World Trade Center. Moved to Woodstock, NY, in 1968, working various jobs. In 1971 moved to the Bay Area. Went to work for the federal Department of Education, and eventually became an officer with the American Federation of Government Employees. He retired in 1995 and lives in Albany, CA.

POLICE DEPT.
JACKSON, MISS
2 1 1 9 4
7-16-61

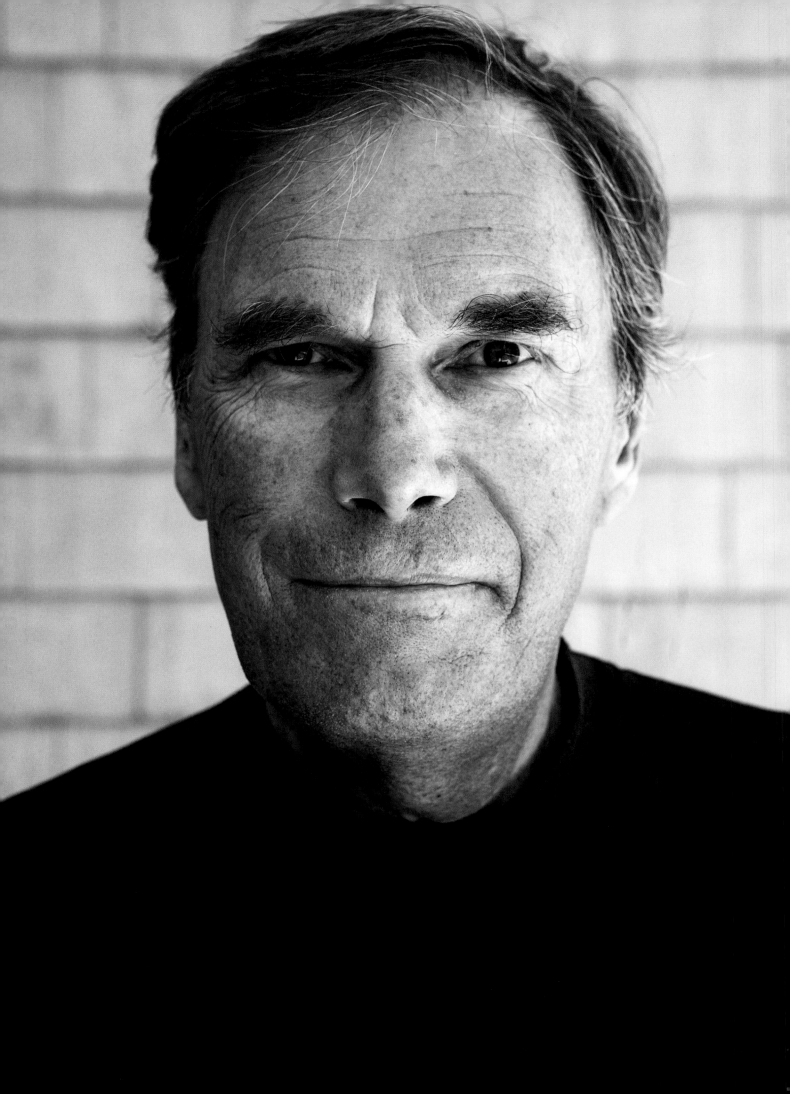

BILL SVANOE

BORN

January 16, 1938, in Wilmington, DE. Grew up in Warren, PA, Northampton, MA, and New York City.

THEN

Graduate student in economics at the University of Minnesota, in Minneapolis. Graduated from Oberlin College in 1959. Active in the 1960 Hubert Humphrey and John Kennedy campaigns.

SINCE THEN

Formed the Rooftop Singers and recorded "Walk Right In," a number-one hit in 1963. Recorded and toured until 1968, when the group disbanded. Began writing plays and screenplays, living in Los Angeles for most of the seventies, and Vail, CO, and Santa Fe, NM, during the eighties. Since 2001 has also taught screenwriting and playwriting at the University of North Carolina, in Chapel Hill.

I was a guitar player and singer. Not a professional one then, but I would organize little sing-alongs. I was very much into the blues, which was not popular then, and I also knew a lot of folk songs, so that would pass the time. In Parchman, I would sing them and conduct sing-alongs.

When we got out they took us to a church, and the Jackson community, mostly the African American community, treated us to a huge dinner. It was a Baptist church, I think, and they were just so grateful for what we'd done, and at that point, the blacks and the whites were all back together, and the men and the women, as opposed to how we had been segregated in prison. I didn't have a guitar with me then, but we did some singing.

When we all came back in the fall for some kind of arraignment, I came down with my twelve-string guitar. At that point, nobody knew about twelve-string guitars.

At the service, we sang "We Shall Overcome," which was quite a moment, because they asked me to lead, playing my guitar. I remember that moment incredibly clear—standing up in front of the church, a church of blacks and whites, and we had all shared an incredible experience. We all felt that things were going to change as a result.

Photographed
June 21, 2007
Kennebunkport, ME
Age: 69

LEWIS ZUCHMAN

- - - - - - - - -

I actually went on the Freedom Rides because of Jackie Robinson.

Robinson was my idol. I was watching the David Susskind TV show ["Open End"] one day and Jackie Robinson was on with Roy Wilkins from the NAACP and Henry [Hank] Thomas, who was one of the original Freedom Riders.

This was just after the bus was bombed in Anniston, and all the other violence in Alabama. Henry Thomas was saying the Rides have to continue. Roy Wilkins was saying no, it's too dangerous. So you had this clash. I wasn't politically sophisticated at all, but to me Jackie Robinson was the true rebel, even though by this time I knew he was a Republican.

On the show there were two or three older African American civil rights leaders, all saying it's too dangerous to continue. And Henry Thomas saying very strongly, we can't back down. Of course, I agreed with Thomas. I didn't understand the politics of any of this, but I felt you can't back down.

Then Jackie Robinson said, "We've got to support this young man," meaning Thomas. I had tears in my eyes. The next morning I went to the CORE office in Manhattan to volunteer.

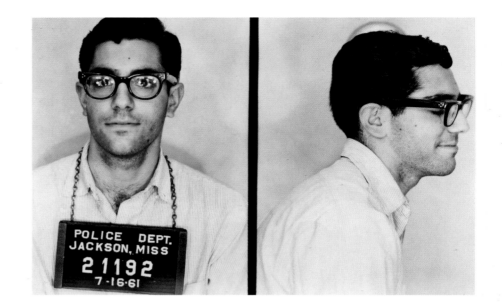

BORN

March 29, 1942, in the Bronx, NY. Grew up in Queens.

THEN

Student at the University of Bridgeport, in Bridgeport, CT.

SINCE THEN

Returned to Bridgeport for a semester and ran the local CORE chapter, then transferred to City College in New York. Walked in James Meredith's March Against Fear in Mississippi in 1966.

After graduating City College in 1967, worked with street gangs in East Harlem and Bushwick, Brooklyn. Later created an Upward Bound basketball program for Puerto Rican and black high school students, which focused on getting its participants into college. Got a master's degree in social work at Columbia University in 1974.

Returned to work in East Harlem, eventually serving as the deputy executive director of the Edwin Gould Services for Children, then the largest black child care agency in the country. Since 1987, has been the executive director of SCAN, the Supportive Children's Advocacy Network. SCAN works with at-risk families in East Harlem and the South Bronx.

Photographed
July 3, 2007
New York, NY
Age: 65

HELEN O'NEAL MCCRAY

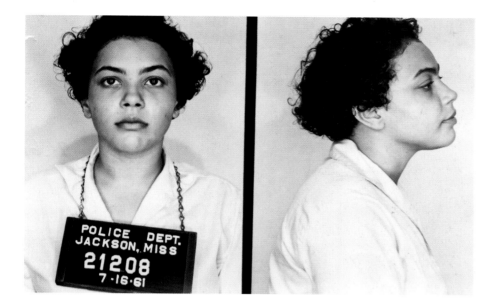

BORN

March 4, 1941, in Clarksdale, MS, and grew up there.

THEN

Sophomore at Jackson State University; dropped out of summer school to join the newly formed Jackson Nonviolent Movement.

SINCE THEN

Continued to volunteer for the movement until she graduated from Jackson State in 1963, then worked for SNCC in Mississippi, developing materials to help illiterate adults learn to read, canvassing for voter registration, and teaching in a Freedom School in McComb, MS, among other projects.

Left Mississippi after Freedom Summer in 1964. Over the next few years lived in New York, Shreveport, LA, and Atlanta, working with various civil rights groups and other nonprofits, including the Law Students for Civil Rights, the Lawyers Constitutional Defense Committee, and the Southern Regional Council.

Moved to Yellow Springs, OH, in 1966. Taught in public elementary schools for twenty-nine years. Since 1999 has taught at Wilberforce University, an historically black school in Wilberforce, OH.

When I decided to drop out of summer school and then get arrested, I wrote my mother and stepfather a letter and dropped it in the mail.

My mother was very displeased. I had wasted money that they really could not afford, and because I withdrew, I could not get any of it back.

My stepfather, well, he probably kept my mother from killing me. [*Laughs.*] My stepfather was very supportive. He thought it was just great what people were doing.

My mother was upset. She worked very hard and I was wasting money. The next three or four times I got arrested I don't think she bothered.

Photographed
November 17, 2006
Yellow Springs, OH
Age: 65

MAY JUN JUL AUG SEP

HAWKINS FIELD, JACKSON AIRPORT

JULY 21

Jackson

James Carey
21219 Berkeley, CA - Age 35

Rev. Francis Geddes
21224 San Francisco, CA - Age 38

Jospeh Gumbiner
21216 Orinda, CA - Age 54 - Died 1993

Mary Jorgensen
21221 Berkeley, CA - Age 45

Russell Jorgensen
21222 Berkeley, CA - Age 44

Rabbi Allan Levine
21217 Bradford, PA - Age 28

Orville Luster
21220 Daly City, CA - Age 36 - Died 2005

Charles Sellers
21223 Berkeley, CA - Age 37

Rev. John Washington
21218 San Francisco, CA - Age 32

GREYHOUND

JULY 21

Nashville to Jackson

Paul Breines
21228 Madison, WI - Age 20

Donna Garde
21226 New York, NY - Age 25

Joel Greenberg
21227 Baltimore, MD - Age 22

Ruth Moskowitz
21225 Brooklyn, NY - Age 25 - Died 1996

178

RUSSELL & MARY JORGENSEN

BORN

Mary was born on July 12, 1916, on a farm outside Bippus, IN, and grew up there. Graduated from Manchester College, in North Manchester, IN.

Russell was born on June 13, 1917, in Racine, WI, and grew up there. Graduated from the University of Wisconsin, in Madison. Was granted conscientious objector status for the draft during WWII.

Russell and Mary met at a hostel in Massachusetts in 1939. They soon married and moved to the west coast, eventually settling in Berkeley, CA, in 1942. Both studied at the Pacific School of Religion, in Berkeley, CA. In 1949, Russell spent a summer working with youth in postwar Japan.

THEN

Russell was a fundraiser for the American Friends Service Committee. They were both members of Fellowship of Reconciliation and active in Berkeley CORE, protesting discrimination in stores and housing.

SINCE THEN

Russell continued to fundraise for the AFSC, which he did until the mid-seventies. He also served on the board of the Pacifica Radio Foundation, and was president of the foundation for a year in 1963. In the mid-sixties, Russell and Mary spent two years in Tanzania, supervising the VISA volunteers in the country.

In 1972, they moved north to help create an intentional community named Monan's Rill, just outside Santa Rosa. They have lived in Nevada City, CA, since 2001.

I had told everybody that if I was going to go to jail, I was going to look like a Southern lady, which I did. And I think this is why Capt. [J. L.] Ray called me in, because he couldn't understand it! I had a hat with a veil, white gloves, white shoes, and a lovely dress, so I felt comfortable going in and talking to him. I'd been arrested a few times already. I wasn't afraid of the police department.

We must have talked for forty-five minutes or an hour. He wanted to know what was going on in Berkeley. He wanted to know why I came. And I told him.

After we'd talked quite a while, I asked him. I said, "Well, what do you like to do when you're not in the police department?" And he said, "I like to go fishing." So I said, "Well, we live in Berkeley, and the wharf's not far from us, and a lot of fishermen there. I guess it's a good catch, and if you want to come up and stay with us, you'd be welcome and go fishing."

He was friendly, asked questions, he really wanted to know. He was not at all like the other people we met in town. I think he'd been softened, because later when we went back to Jackson with many other Freedom Riders to get arraigned, he was in the police line; and people were so friendly to him and shaking hands, I heard he had to leave the police line. I think it just got to him, and he knew that it was wrong what was happening.

—Mary Jorgensen

Photographed
February 20, 2007
Nevada City, CA
Ages: 89 and 90

CHARLES SELLERS

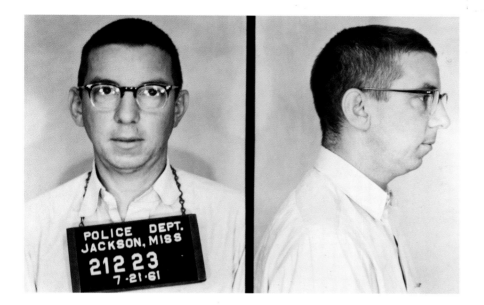

POLICE DEPT.
JACKSON, MISS
21223
7·21·61

BORN

September 9, 1923, in Charlotte, NC, and grew up there. Served three years in the army during World War II, then graduated Harvard in 1947. Got his Ph.D. in American history at University of North Carolina, in Chapel Hill, in 1950; active locally on racial issues.

THEN

History professor, University of California, Berkeley. Active in the local CORE chapter, challenging discrimination in stores and housing, among other targets. Also very involved in the Free Speech Movement, which began in 1964.

SINCE THEN

Taught at Berkeley until he retired in 1990. Is the author of *The Market Revolution: Jacksonian America, 1815–46,* and a two-volume biography of James K. Polk, the second of which won the Bancroft Prize. Still lives in Berkeley, and travels frequently with his wife on birding and camping trips.

When I was in high school, I went to an NAACP meeting in a black church, which was packed with three or four hundred people. An imposing gentleman, who was introduced as Bishop Gordon of the AME Zion Church, got up and preached the most powerful sermon I had ever heard.

I was one of only two or three white people in this enormous congregation and I guess this was a "scales falling from my eyes" kind of experience that I never got over. I was in dissent with my society from that time on.

Photographed
February 16, 2007
Berkeley, CA
Age: 83

PAUL BREINES

When I was a freshman at the University of Wisconsin, I pledged a fraternity. At a pledge dinner, I got up and said, "Hey, these students [in the South] are sitting in. Have you been reading about this?" I had a hat for the occasion. I said, "I want to pass around a hat and raise some money. I'm not sure where we send it, but I think they could use some funds, and I'll find out." My pledge father knocked the hat out of my hand and called me a nigger lover.

I soon met a girl, whom I subsequently married. She was a left-winger from New York. She said, "What is that on your sweater?" I said, "That's a pledge pin." She said, "What?" I said, "What's wrong?" She said, "Don't you know what fraternities are?" My education was beginning.

She had enormous impact on me: "What don't you change your life? Why are you such a jerk with a pledge pin and hanging out with these dodos? What about the Socialist Club?" I said, "Socialist Club? What's that?" Soon I was on picket lines at the Woolworth's in Madison, being called a nigger lover again, being told to go back to the Soviet Union.

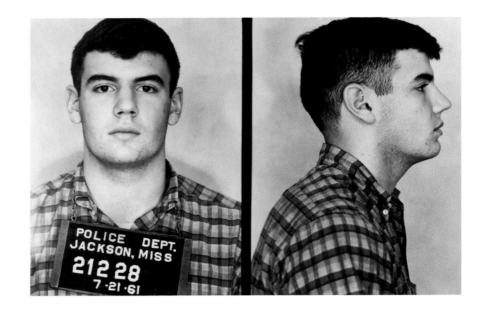

BORN
April 16, 1941, in Manhattan. Grew up in Queens and Scarsdale, NY.

THEN
Sophomore at the University of Wisconsin, in Madison. Had participated in several civil rights demonstrations.

SINCE THEN
Graduated Wisconsin in 1963, then got a Ph.D. in European intellectual history there in 1972. Continued to be active in the civil rights movement and later in the anti-war movement. Has been a professor at Boston College since 1975, teaching courses on modern European intellectual history and the history of gender and sexuality.

Photographed
June 20, 2007
Boston, MA
Age: 66

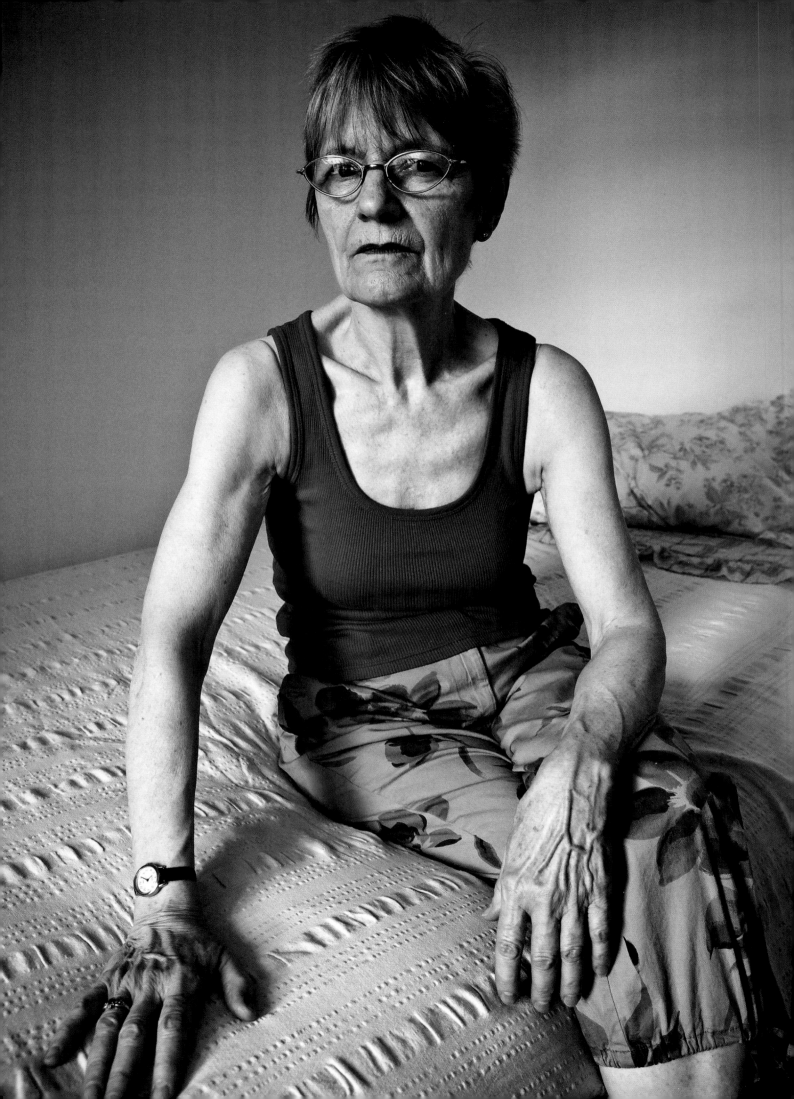

DONNA GARDE

My family was a regular, New England family.

We had conversations about the corn and how many jars of jam we'd put up. In Parchman, we shared the mail that we got in the cellblock. People would read their letters. I read my letter, and it said, "Dad planted ten rows of corn, and the corn's really good this year, and grandma's fine, and blah, blah, blah."

Somebody said, what does it mean? Are these codes? This is code, right?

And I said, no, this is real. It was so funny because other people were much more sophisticated; this was the summer of the Berlin crisis, and people had even set up different codes for their letters meaning East Berlin or West Berlin.

BORN
December 29, 1935, in Middletown, CT. Grew up in Cromwell, CT.

THEN
Living in Westfield, NJ, and teaching at an elementary school there. Had graduated from Syracuse University in 1957.

SINCE THEN
Returned to Mississippi in 1964 as part of Freedom Summer, teaching in a Freedom School near Meridian, MS.

Has spent her career primarily as a teacher, working, among other places, in an elementary school in Spanish Harlem and in a program for welfare mothers on the Lower East Side. In the 1970s earned a master's degree in special education at Columbia University, and taught in special education for several years. Later taught remedial English at the City University of New York and other colleges. Today teaches English as a second language in three different institutions. Also worked for ten years as a freelance technical writer for businesses.

Photographed
June 27, 2006
New York, NY
Age: 70

TRAILWAYS

JULY 23

Nashville to Jackson

Albert Huddleson

21236 San Francisco, CA - Age 32 - Died 1975

Candida Lall

21238 Larkspur, CA - Age 18

Morton Linder

21234 San Francisco, CA - Age 23

Peggi Oakley

21237 San Francisco, CA - Age 22

Michael Powell

21239 San Jose, CA - Age 20

Alexander Weiss

21235 San Francisco, CA - Age 25

Ralph Williams

21240 San Francisco, CA - Age 36 - Died 1985

HAWKINS FIELD, JACKSON AIRPORT

JULY 24

Montgomery to Jackson

Alphonso Petway

21241 Montgomery, AL - Age 16

Kredelle Petway

21242 Montgomery, AL - Age 20

Rev. Matthew Petway

21244 Montgomery, AL - Age 46 - Died 1972

Cecil Thomas

21243 Albany, CA - Age 44 - Died 1969

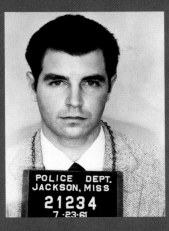

MORTON LINDER

When I got out of jail and went back to Philadelphia, that's when I tried to figure out why I had gone.
I read Gandhi and I read Martin Luther King, and tried to set in my mind why I had been there in the first place.

I think it was a feeling of—maybe of guilt, maybe obligation. I did feel it was a window of time when I could do something. I didn't have my veterinary license and couldn't practice yet and it was just a window of time when I could do something like that. Maybe I wouldn't have a chance to put my body on the line later on.

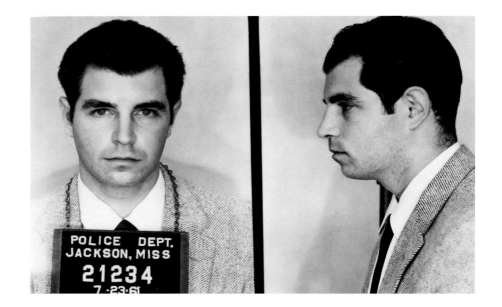

BORN
January 30, 1938, in Philadelphia, and grew up there.

THEN
Newly arrived in San Francisco, CA. Had just graduated from the veterinary school at the University of Pennsylvania.

SINCE THEN
A practicing veterinarian in the Haight-Ashbury neighborhood of San Francisco and active in CORE demonstrations, the anti-war movement, and local development issues.

In 1969 moved with his wife to Point Reyes, CA, where they still live. Practiced veterinary medicine part-time and also worked for several years as a mechanic in a local bicycle shop. Now retired. He and his wife have been to every Burning Man since 2000.

Photographed
February 18, 2007
Point Reyes, CA
Age: 69

PEGGI OAKLEY

POLICE DEPT.
JACKSON, MISS
21237
7·23·61

We were interviewed by an FBI agent at some point after being arrested. That was kind of strange.

He wanted to know, "Why are you doing this?"

I said something about defending some amendment. I can't even remember—I keep thinking the 14th Amendment, but I don't know if that's the appropriate one or not.

He said, "Don't you know nobody believes in those things anymore?"

BORN
October 21, 1938, in Darby, PA, and grew up there.

THEN
Had just moved to San Francisco from New York City, where she had moved in 1959 after dropping out of Houghton College, in western New York State. In New York had worked for the National Council of Churches and taken classes at the New School for Social Research. (She is listed in the records as Margaret Ihra; Margaret is her given name, and she was married at the time.)

SINCE THEN
Lived briefly in Miami and New York, then returned to San Francisco to live with Alexander Weiss, whom she had met during training for the Freedom Rides. Active in CORE. Spent ten months in 1967–68 with Weiss and their two children traveling around Europe in a VW van.

Separated from Weiss in 1970. Returned to college and graduated San Francisco State in 1975. Started a typesetting and word-processing business in 1980, which she ran until she retired in 2003. Has also volunteered frequently at the Haight-Asbury Switchboard.

Photographed
February 14, 2007
San Francisco, CA
Age: 68

ALEXANDER WEISS

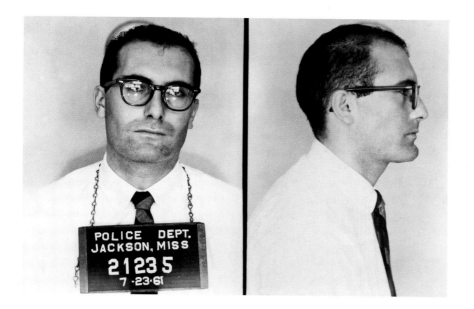

POLICE DEPT.
JACKSON, MISS
21235
7·23·61

BORN

May 16, 1936, in Vienna. Escaped Austria with his parents and sister, via Trieste, in 1940. His family resettled in San Francisco later that year.

THEN

Student, San Francisco State. Served in the Navy 1955–57.

SINCE THEN

Direct-action chairman for San Francisco CORE 1961–64. Moved in with Peggi Oakley, whom he had met while training for the Freedom Rides. Worked as a keeper at the San Francisco Zoo 1964–67. Traveled for ten months in Europe with Peggi and their two children in a VW Camper.

Returned to San Francisco. In 1970 he and Peggi separated. Also that year he became a state park ranger, working in various parks in and around the Bay Area, including Candlestick Point State Recreation Area, where he was chief ranger.

Initiated a successful campaign to save the Angel Island Immigration Station from being torn down. The station, on the largest island in San Francisco Bay, served as a point of entry into the country for thousands of immigrants, especially Asians, from 1910–40.

Retired as a park ranger in 1987, and returned to the zoo as a keeper for eight more years. Now lives in Oakland with his wife and works on an as-needed basis for Alameda County, helping run elections.

I grew up in the Fillmore District, which was like the Harlem of San Francisco, but at the time it was fairly mixed. It was primarily black, but lots of refugees. There was a little Jewish section with Jewish delis. I had black buddies at school. In the navy I had a lot of black shipmates who were buddies.

Once all this stuff started happening down South, I just couldn't believe it. One of the motivations for joining CORE and volunteering to go on the Freedom Rides was I did not want to be one of those "good Germans who just looked the other way."

I talked to my father. I said, "I want to go." He was totally against it. "You're gonna get killed. It's not us this time, it's the Schwartzes."

I said, "Hey, you know, this is what happened to you. I'm not gonna stand by."

Photographed
February 17, 2007
Oakland, CA
Age: 70

KREDELLE PETWAY

– – – – – – – – –

My dad discussed the idea of going to Jackson with us— me and my two brothers.
It was somewhat of an abbreviated training session in nonviolence. Then he asked each of us, "With knowing what we're about and what we want to accomplish and what we want to do, what would be your reaction?"

I've never been a person to start anything physical or be confrontational, so I said I would not do anything that would jeopardize what we were going to do.

Then he asked my older brother, "What would you do if somebody hit you." He said, "I'd try to knock their head off." [*Laughs.*]

My father said, "Okay, you can't go."

My younger brother [Alphonso] at that time was sixteen. I guess after my older brother's answer, he knew what his answer needed to be. [*Laughs.*]

BORN
June 9, 1941, in Camden, AL. Grew up in Pensacola, FL.

THEN
Junior, Florida A & M University, in Tallahassee. Active in the civil rights movement. Arrested along with her father, Rev. Matthew Petway, and her younger brother, Alphonso.

SINCE THEN
Graduated FAMU. Worked for the Department of Veterans Affairs in St. Petersburg, FL, from 1967 to 1973, when she moved to Louisville, KY. Worked there for the Urban League, the IRS as an auditor, and then returned to the Department of Veteran Affairs, eventually transferring back to St. Petersburg in 1986. In 2001 went to work for H&R Block, managing an office there until she retired in 2006. Now lives in Apollo Beach, FL.

Photographed
May 1, 2007
Apollo Beach, FL
Age: 65

ALPHONSO PETWAY

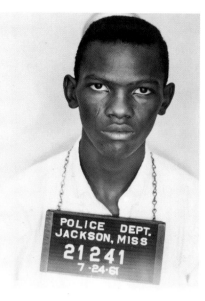

- - - - - - - - -

I wanted to be involved.
I wanted to participate in my own
freedom. That was the kind of
statement I made to my daddy,
that I wanted to participate in my
own struggle.

BORN

January 28, 1945, in Camden, AL. Grew up in Pensacola, FL, and Montgomery.

THEN

Sophomore in high school. Had spent a week with his father, Rev. Matthew
Petway, studying civil disobedience at Highlander Folk School in Tennessee.
Arrested along with his father and his older sister, Kredelle.

SINCE THEN

Moved to Louisville, KY, with his family in 1962. Worked with his father
establishing a new chapter of the NAACP in Louisville. Became a minister in
1967. Was one of the national organizers for Martin Luther King Jr.'s Poor
People's Campaign in 1968.

Served as pastor for a number of churches in Kentucky, New Jersey, and
Mississippi. Since 2006 has worked as a chaplain for a company providing
in-home hospice care in Mobile, AL.

Photographed
March 27, 2007
Mobile, AL
Age: 62

GREYHOUND

JULY 29

Nashville to Jackson

Byron Baer
21256 Englewood, NJ - Age 31 - Died 2007

Hilmar Pabel
21253 Munich, Germany - Age 50 - Died 2000

Catherine Prensky
21252 Madison, WI - Age 18

Sally Rowley
21251 New York, NY - Age 29

Judith Scroggins
21250 Cincinnati, OH - Age 18

Rick Sheviakov
21254 Berkeley, CA - Age 18

Woollcott Smith
21255 East Lansing, MI - Age 20

Ellen Ziskind
21249 New York, NY - Age 21

BYRON BAER

BORN

October 18, 1929, in Pittsburgh.

THEN

Special effects technician working in TV and the movies, living in Englewood, NJ. Had attended Cornell for several years but had dropped out. Before going to Mississippi, had made a small transistor radio to smuggle into Parchman. While in Parchman, was one of many people who made chess sets out of bread or other available materials. A photograph of his chess set, smuggled out of Parchman by Robert Rogers, is on page 240.

SINCE THEN

Participated in the Selma-to-Montgomery march in 1965. A member of CORE and very involved with fair-housing efforts and school desegregation in Englewood. Beginning in 1971 served eleven consecutive terms in the New Jersey state assembly. Elected to the state senate in 1993 and served there until he resigned in 2005 for health reasons.

DIED

June 25, 2007.

Photographed
June 6, 2007
Englewood, NJ
Age: 77

WOOLLCOTT SMITH

BORN

June 9, 1941, in Baltimore, MD. Grew up primarily in East Lansing, MI.

THEN

Sophomore, Michigan State University, East Lansing.

SINCE THEN

Graduated Michigan State in 1963, then did graduate work there and at Johns Hopkins University in Baltimore, earning his doctorate in 1969. Active in efforts to get Johns Hopkins to recruit more minorities to be graduate students. Also active in anti-war protests. Since 1981 has taught statistics at Temple University, in Philadelphia.

Byron Baer had made this radio to smuggle into Parchman. He showed it to me in Nashville. It was totally homemade—an earpiece, a very long thin wire that was the aerial, and transistors and a hearing-aid battery embedded in a smooth oblong piece of plastic.

In Nashville we were experimenting with it. Byron somehow smuggled into the jail in Jackson outside his body cavities. The big issue there was getting it supposited for the transfer to Parchman. He wrapped the aerial around the transistors, and then wrapped the whole thing in two rubbers.

He got it out and working as soon as we got to Parchman, in the first offenders camp. The only radio station he could pick up was one of these low-power country stations licensed only for the daytime. At sunset, it had to go off the air. We were running around with this very thin wire that was, let's say, 100 feet long. People had their arms up in the air. [*Laughs.*]

We'd do it down as far away as we could from the observation station, where the guards were, but for all practical purposes it was out in the open.

The big thing it helped was keeping track of the home-run race between Mantle and Maris. The Catholic priest and the rabbi would come in and give us news of the race, but we already knew. We'd have to say, "Oh, yeah, that's interesting."

Photographed
June 19, 2007
Woods Hole, MA
Age: 66

201

ELLEN ZISKIND

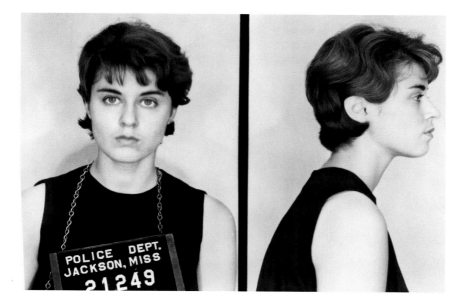

BORN

September 5, 1939, in Lowell, MA, and grew up there.

THEN

Student, School of General Studies at Columbia University, in New York City. Had earlier attended Antioch College, in Yellow Springs, OH, for three years. Worked as a volunteer at the CORE office in New York for several weeks before going to Jackson.

SINCE THEN

Graduated Columbia in 1962, later got a master's degree in social work from Simmons College, in Boston. Since 1977 she has been a practicing psychotherapist in Brookline, MA, where she lives.

What really got me to go, aside from my belief in what people were doing, were the young black men I met while working in the CORE office, men from Mississippi who had been on the front lines. They were young. They'd been kicked and beaten and jailed. They were really Christian and they were really dedicated to nonviolence, even if they weren't in their entire lives but in terms of their participation in the movement.

I had never met anybody like them. They were completely uncynical. They believed in democracy in a way I never thought about it. They believed in things I took for granted and they were willing to die for it and there was something—I start to cry when I think of these men. There was something about them and their sweetness, their commitment.

Because I went as late as I did in the summer I knew there was a woman at Parchman who would give us vaginal searches and have no rubber gloves on. Actually, by the time I got there she was wearing rubber gloves.

Photographed
July 11, 2007
Brookline, MA
Age: 67

ILLINOIS CENTRAL TRAIN STATION

JULY 30

New Orleans to Jackson

Albert Barouh
21261 Los Angeles, CA - Age 21 - Died 1961

Winston Fuller
21263 Los Angeles, CA - Age 24

Joseph Gerbac
21258 Los Angeles, CA - Age 21

Michael Grubbs
21271 Los Angeles, CA - Age 24

Alan Kaufman
21264 Berkeley, CA - Age 21

William Leons
21267 Los Angeles, CA - Age 25

Herbert Mann
21268 Los Angeles, CA - Age 35 - Died 2003

Max Pavesic
21270 Los Angeles, CA - Age 21

Philip Posner
21269 Los Angeles, CA - Age 22

Helen Singleton
21260 Los Angeles, CA - Age 28

Robert Singleton
21265 Los Angeles, CA - Age 25

Richard Steward
21257 New Orleans, CA - Age 21

Lonnie Thurman
21262 Los Angeles, CA - Age 34

Sam Joe Townsend
21266 Los Angeles, CA - Age 27 - Died 1971

Tanya Wren
21259 Los Angeles, CA - Age 22

MAX PAVESIC

We were in maximum security in Parchman.

There was a black trustee that would bring the meals on a cart, escorted by a guard. The trustee had to keep his hands on the cart, and the guard would slip the tray in through the slot to us. Alan [Kaufman] was lying on a cot towards the bars with his hands open. All of a sudden, there were three or four cigarettes—Lucky Strikes—and a pack of matches that trustee passed so fast I didn't see him. Alan didn't see him. The guard didn't see him, and he was standing right there in front of him. Alan was so shocked I leaned over and closed his hand.

Those were the only smokes we had the whole time we were incarcerated and everybody smoked in those days. Boy, a couple of drags after we hadn't smoked for—it just knocked us right on our ass. We were higher then kites. [*Laughs.*]

BORN

August 25, 1939, in Chicago. Grew up there and in Los Angeles, where his family moved in 1949. Childhood friends with Joseph Gerbac in Chicago.

THEN

Junior, UCLA. Active in protests against ROTC and the House Un-American Activities Committee, among other causes.

SINCE THEN

Graduated UCLA in 1962, then did his graduate work at the University of Colorado, Boulder. Taught archaeology and anthropology at Idaho State University, in Pocatello, from 1967 until 1973, when he moved to Boise State University. Retired in 2001. Now lives in Portland, OR.

Photographed
February 23, 2007
Portland, OR
Age: 67

JOSEPH GERBAC

Every summer I used to work as a truck driver.
I had an in with the union so I delivered beer in LA. But there was a strike or something that year and business was bad, so I went down to San Diego, where Greg—I call him Greg [Max Pavesic]—was on a dig with the UCLA archaeology group.

I spent a week with those guys. There was some other guy that talked Greg into going on the Freedom Ride. I never planned on going. I went to the party the night before they left and someone was going around, "Hey, we got one more ticket for Mississippi. Someone flaked out." I had been drinking and whatever, so I said, "Okay. I'll go."

I wrote a note to my parents and gave somebody my car keys and they brought my car back to my parents' house and the next thing I knew I was on a plane, with a hangover, going to New Orleans.

BORN
October 14, 1939, in Chicago. Grew up there and in Los Angeles, where his family moved in 1952. Childhood friends with Max Pavesic in Chicago.

THEN
Junior at UCLA.

SINCE THEN
Graduated UCLA in 1962, and then UCLA law school in 1965. Worked as a public defender in Los Angeles for three years. Has been a solo practitioner ever since, first in Los Angeles and, since 1985, in Lompoc, CA. He lives in Solvang, CA.

Photographed
February 7, 2007
Lompoc, CA
Age: 67

WILLIAM LEONS

BORN

August 29, 1935, in Rotterdam, the Netherlands, and grew up there. His parents were both involved in the Resistance during World War II. His father, a paper salesman, provided newsprint to the underground; his mother hid refugees trying to escape Holland. His father was arrested in 1942 and sent to Mauthausen, a concentration camp in Austria, where he was later killed. His mother was arrested in 1943 and sent to Vught, a concentration camp in the Netherlands. She was liberated in late 1944. He and his mother immigrated to the United States in 1949, living in Hoboken, NJ.

THEN

Graduate student in anthropology at UCLA, where he had done his undergraduate work. Active in civil rights, picketing at various shops and stores in Los Angeles.

SINCE THEN

Got his master's degree at UCLA, then a Ph.D. at Penn State in 1969. Continued to be active in the civil rights movement and also in the anti-war movement. Taught at Goucher College, in Baltimore, MD. Since 1975 has taught at the University of Toledo, in Ohio. He lives in Maumee, OH.

Photographed
November 16, 2006
Maumee, OH
Age: 71

HELEN SINGLETON

We went directly into the white waiting room and sat on the bench there. The policeman simply said, "Are y'all gonna move?" He asked us one more time, and we didn't. We were taken to the city jail. The person booking us was using what looked like an elementary school composition book.

He said, "What school do you go to?"

I said, "Santa Monica City College."

He said, "How do you spell Santa Monica?"

I was young at the time and thought he should know how to spell.

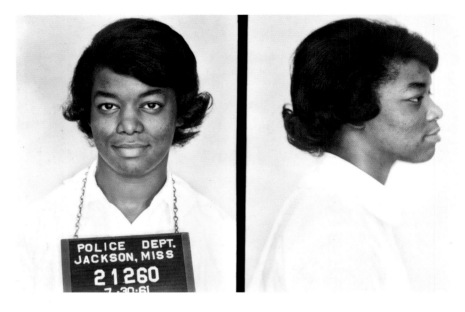

BORN
November 27, 1932, in Philadelphia and grew up there.

THEN
Freshman, Santa Monica City College. Had married Robert Singleton in 1955.

SINCE THEN
Transferred to UCLA, alternating college with child-raising, and graduated in 1974 with a major in fine arts. Got a master's degree in public administration in 1985 from Loyola Marymount University, and then worked at UCLA developing courses, special programs, and symposia on the arts and humanities. In 1992 began working as a consultant for arts groups, including the California Arts Council, the Los Angeles County Museum of Art, and the Missouri Arts Council, among others. Retired in 1999, and lives in Inglewood, CA, with her husband.

Photographed
August 19, 2005
Los Angeles, CA
Age: 72

ROBERT SINGLETON

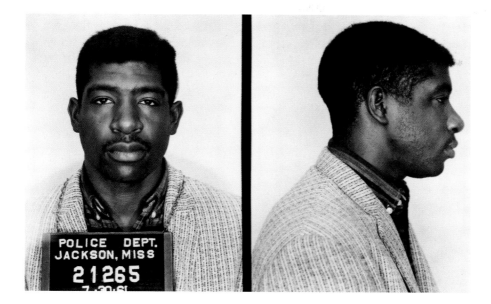

POLICE DEPT.
JACKSON, MISS
21265

BORN

January 8, 1936, in Philadelphia and grew up there.

THEN

Graduate student in economics at University of California, Los Angeles, where he had also studied as an undergraduate. Head of the NAACP chapter on campus; active in protests against discrimination in housing and employment, among other targets. Had married Helen Singleton in 1955.

SINCE THEN

Organized a CORE chapter in Santa Monica, CA. Got his Ph.D. in 1964, and taught at UCLA for a few years after the NAACP chapter was kicked off by the administration; was the first director of the Black Studies Center at UCLA. Became a professor of economics at Loyola Marymount University in Los Angeles, where he was head of the department for twenty years and still teaches. Lives in Inglewood, CA, with his wife.

We were arrested immediately and put in the paddy wagon.
That was interesting. There was one fellow by the name of Alan Kaufman, I haven't seen him since then. He and I were sitting next to each other. A policeman came up on the side and looked in the window and said to me, "You're a black son of a bitch, ain't you?"

I said to him, "Isn't that a beautiful color?"

And he just froze. He didn't know how to respond to that. Alan Kaufman just patted me on the back.

Photographed
Aug. 19, 2005
Los Angeles, CA
Age: 69

RICHARD STEWARD

Jerome Smith was a friend I'd grown up with. We were running buddies, if you know what I mean. We did a lot of . . . things together. We lost track of each other, but when I found out about the Freedom Rides, I discovered he was helping organize the effort in New Orleans. I told him I wanted to be a Freedom Rider.

"You do something nonviolent?" he said. "That's a laugh."

I insisted. He said, "You'll need training." I said fine.

Then he slapped me real hard.

"OK," he said. "You've been trained."

BORN
December 12, 1939, in New Orleans, and grew up there.

THEN
Junior, Dillard University, New Orleans.

SINCE THEN
Graduated Dillard in 1962 and moved to Los Angeles, working and doing graduate studies in education at USC. Organized the black student union at USC in the late 1960s. Taught in the public schools, primarily middle school and junior high, from 1969 until he retired in 1997.

Photographed
August 25, 2005
Los Angeles, CA
Age: 65

TRAILWAYS

AUGUST 13

Jackson

George Raymond
21316 New Orleans, LA - Age 18 - Died 1973

Pauline Sims
21315 Putney, England - Age 22

TRAILWAYS

SEPTEMBER 13

New Orleans to Jackson

Rev. Gilbert Avery
21366 Roxbury, MA - Age 30

Rev. Myron Bloy, Jr.
21363 Cambridge, MA - Age 35 - Died 1985

Rev. James Breeden
21368 Boston, MA - Age 26

Rev. John Crocker, Jr.
21362 Providence, RI - Age 37

Rev. James Evans
21367 St. Clair, MO - Age 31

Rev. John Evans
21369 Toledo, OH - Age 36

Rev. Quinland Gordon
21372 Washington, DC - Age 45 - Died 1990

Rev. James Jones
21371 Chicago, IL - Age 34

Rev. John Morris
21364 Atlanta, GA - Age 31

Rev. Robert Pierson
21361 New York, NY - Age 35 - Died 1997

Rev. Geoffrey Simpson
21365 Pewaukee, WI - Age 29

Rev. Robert Taylor
21373 Chicago, IL - Age 29 - Died 1999

Rev. William Wendt
21359 Washington, DC - Age 41 - Died 2001

Rev. Vernon Woodward
21370 Cincinnati, OH - Age 27

Rev. Merrill Young
21360 Boston, MA - Age 31

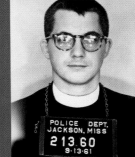

REV. JOHN CROCKER, JR.

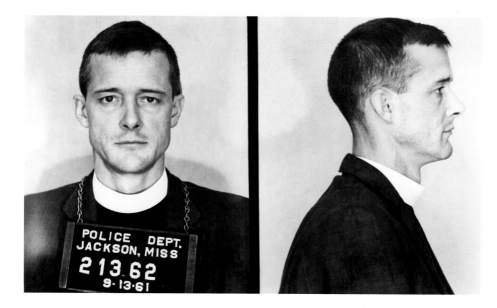

BORN

October 19, 1923, in Oxford, England. Grew up primarily in Princeton, NJ. Went to college at Harvard, leaving to serve in the navy during World War II, then graduated in 1946. Did his seminary studies at Episcopal Divinity School in Cambridge, MA.

THEN

Episcopal Chaplain at Brown University, in Providence, RI.

SINCE THEN

Later served as the Episcopal Chaplain at MIT, in Cambridge, MA. Now retired and lives in Providence, RI.

- - - - - - - - -

We were these little conservative Episcopal clergymen with round collars on, and we were the least revolutionary people you could imagine. The reason we got arrested was that we were simply sitting in the bus terminal in Jackson and we were operating under what was then the federal law. It was Jackson that was breaking the law. We were just a bunch of pussycats.

We did our thing, which was to get arrested. That was no hardship to me. The Jackson officials and police asked us, "Why did you come down here to mess us up? You're New Englanders."

"Well, I'm sorry," I said. "I thought I was an American first."

They threw us in jail. The first job that needed to be done was cleaning the toilets, and I was an expert toilet cleaner. And then in the middle of the night when we wanted to communicate—they segregated blacks from whites—we communicated by singing hymns at the top of our lungs. We could just hear them off in the distance and they us.

Photographed
June 18, 2007
West Kingston, RI
Age: 83

FREEDOM Riders
Come! - See! - Hear!
Second
Return of Freedom Riders
MASS MEETING
Sunday, Sept. 10th
8:30 P. M.
at the
Masonic Temple
Guest Speaker
REV. C. T. VIVIAN
One of the First Riders,   Pastor of Cosmopolitan Community Church of Chattanooga, Tenn.

Also Charles Earl Cox, Jackson Freedom Riders

Sponsored by: Jackson Non-Violent Movement
1104 Lynch Street

The Jackson Nonviolent Movement staged a mass meeting in mid-August and a second one in September when large numbers of Freedom Riders, having bailed out and left the state, had to return to Jackson. They came back to appear in court and get a date for new trial.

EXTENDED INTERVIEWS

JAMES LAWSON

See page 36

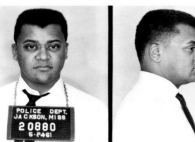

WHEN WE STARTED OUT, WE started out on the same route as CORE had designed. Our intention was that no matter how many people got beat up, we'd have another crew. If we got beat up in Jackson, we'd put another crew into Jackson who would go from Jackson to whatever the next stop was. That was the notion.

But as the arrests took place in Jackson, and as we saw their effect, we decided to put out the cry and let people get arrested in Jackson and go after filling up the jails. That then became the strategy. So the arrests in Jackson prompted us to make another adjustment, and in many ways that was just as good.

We also realized we were going to put Jackson and Mississippi at center stage. Mississippi was a closed society. The Sovereignty Commission, the KKK, the White Citizens' Council were all very much in control. They were tyrannizing whites and blacks who might in any way blink on the issues.

The movement had had very little inroads there. Medgar Evers was just beginning his work; the Freedom Ride gave him backbone. But it also gave a number of other black folk in the city backbone. Within the first twenty-four hours I was there, one of my long-term friends and mentors, Clare Collins of the Collins Funeral Home, organized Churchwomen United in Jackson, and they sent us little care packages—toothbrush, toothpaste, and I don't know what else. But that in itself was a chink in the armor of segregation in Jackson.

I could recognize this because I'd been in and out of Jackson on two or three previous occasions. I did a workshop in 1959 in Jackson on non-violence. Martin King did the session one afternoon and then he spoke to a mass meeting that night. At the mass meeting, the large auditorium was half-full. King was not going anywhere in the country at that time without having standing-room-only crowds. That's what was happening, literally, all over the country. Yet in Jackson the auditorium was maybe half-full. I'll never forget that. So I knew how scared the black community was, how vulnerable they felt in that state and that city. ■

JEAN THOMPSON

See page 38

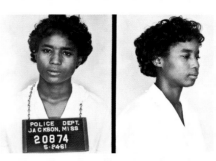

I THINK WE WERE IN THE CITY jail for a day, and then we went to the county jail for a day, and then we were transferred to the county penal farm. The city jail wasn't the best thing. It had bugs, and I was afraid of bugs. There were praying mantises, which I was afraid of, and spiders. But you had to show that you were strong, I had learned, so I didn't show any fear.

And then some people bailed out, and we started thinning out. And we went to the county jail, which was plush compared to the city jail. Fewer bugs, and county had bunks, I think.

By the time we got to the penal farm, I was the only female left. And when we got there, we were interrogated. We were told that these are the rules and the regulations. And one of the rules was that you always have to say "yes, sir" and "no, sir."

My parents, especially my mother, taught us you don't have to say "yes, sir" and "no, sir" to white people. You give your respect but you can always say "no" and go on. And I was determined that I was not gonna say "no, sir" or "yes, sir"—the other part of that was "yes'm" and "no'sah." We didn't say that in my house.

The superintendent started asking me questions. I would say yes or no and avoid the "sir" by immediately continuing with my answer—no, and blah, blah, blah. We were in a little room just the two of us, and he was six feet tall, and he must have weighed 200 and some pounds. I was slender at that time, and I weighed ninety pounds.

We're sitting at a table. And he came up with a question, and he

REV. C.T. VIVIAN

See page 40

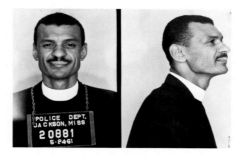

must have bumped the table or something. I turned around, and I wasn't quick enough. So I just said no, and sort of paused. And he slapped me so hard that I saw stars. I must have been unconscious for two or three seconds.

It went over briefly, and in a couple of seconds I was able to readjust. But I know I was unconscious for a while 'cause I remember blackness. But after that one slap I decided I'm not gonna get hit again 'cause I may not last. But he wasn't able to catch me anymore and he got tired, so he just said let her go, bring on someone else.

Then someone bailed out and reported that I and others had been hit. They brought the FBI in to investigate. They interviewed me. They interviewed the superintendent, and all the other people. And they concluded that nothing had happened. No one was beaten.

Well, I must be hallucinating now 'cause I know I felt that man's hand on my face. I know I heard other people being whacked. But nothing happened. That said a lot to me about what actually happens in this country. It was very eye-opening. ■

THE NORMAL WHITE RESPONSE IS that we were creating violence. Some of them jeered at the idea of our being nonviolent. No, you're not nonviolent. You actually are creating the violence. If you would just be, you know, quiet Niggs—I mean, colored people, then there wouldn't be any violence.

Any dictator doesn't want anybody to say anything about his dictatorship, because obviously, he's going to create violence, but then, also obviously, he's going to blame it on the victim. We didn't play that game.

That was not only a white line but also a scared black line: "Oh, please don't bother these white people. Because they're gonna going to be violent. They're gonna kill us. They're gonna kill us. They're gonna kill us."

What these liberal white fellows in the South were saying is that the non-liberals down here are gonna kill you, and you know we're not gonna say anything to them, and we won't be able to help you. This is the unspoken stuff now. And without our help, why, you could never make it, because you must have us talking to white people. And we were saying, that's your importance, all right, but you haven't freed nobody.

This is the genius of Martin, who spoke the whole thing so well, week after week, month after month, from that time on. Until we are in charge of our own freedom, there is not gonna be any freedom for us. As long as we allow someone else to speak for us, and they know each other very well, there's not gonna be a breaking of the old order. We're still going to be killed whenever any policeman

decides to. And they are always gonna be covered up if they care to cover it up at all.

Who's going to get honest enough to cut through this? This is who we are. We know we can be killed in the process. So? We're gonna get killed anyway. But we're not going to do it without it being obvious, and we're not going to do it without it being all over the world, and we're not going to do it playing the game of your so-called democracy, which is undemocratic. ■

BERNARD LAFAYETTE, JR.

See page 40

HANK THOMAS

See page 50

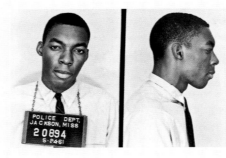

I WAS ABOUT SEVEN. THE CITY transportation system in Tampa, Florida, was segregated. You would get on in the front of the streetcar, and put your money in the receptacle, then you would get off and go to the back, where there was another door.

There was actually a partition inside the streetcar—just in front of the back door. So when you entered the back door you're already in the segregated section. It got pretty crowded back there and people would stand up.

This particular time I was with my grandmother and we put the money in to the receptacle and we started to the back. Well you had to run because sometimes they would fold the steps up and close the doors and take off with your money. So there was always anxiety when you had to get on.

Some people would run so they could catch the door. I did. I ran and I caught the door and was holding it. My grandmother was also running and she had on high heel shoes and the heel of her shoe got caught in the cracks of the cobblestone around the tracks and she fell. I tried to reach back for her and hold the door, which was impossible.

I felt really torn, like a sword cut me in half. I remember that feeling even now. I said to myself, "When I get grown I'm going to do something about this." ∎

EARLY ON, I NOTICED MY MOTHER always refer to white people as "Mr." and "Mrs." But when the insurance man came to our house, he always referred to my aunt—I lived with my aunt—by her first name. My aunt's first name was Rebecca, and he would say, "Rebecca." And my first act of rebellion I can remember was to say to the insurance man, "You mean Mrs. Williams, don't you?"

I was probably nine, ten years old.

And he'd looked at me a little bit strange and got into the conversation again. I had to correct him about three times and then he would say, "Okay, Ms. Williams."

Rebellion came natural to me. There are people in my family who were naturally rebellious, and there were people in my family who had to leave a certain city because one of the men had challenged the white folks for what they were doing. So when I learned about this about my family, later on as an adult, I realized that this is something that came natural to me. I just had that natural sense that this is not the way things supposed to be.

I did my own little things in St. Augustine as an act of rebellion. If I had been in any other Southern city, I would've suffered bodily harm. I would go to the city library, where you weren't supposed to go, and they would not give me books. So I started taking my own book, just to sit there for about an hour, just sit there and read. The police weren't called. Folks knew me. And nobody bothered me.

That's why I kinda got a reputation—folks thought I was crazy.

There was a small transit bus company in St. Augustine whose riders were primarily blacks. I never rode in the back of those particular buses, and nobody ever said anything. It was never an issue. 'Course, blacks automatically went to the back. But I never would do that. Then again, by then everybody knew old crazy Henry Thomas. [*Laughs.*]

At the time of the Montgomery bus boycott [1955-56] I talked to a few of the ministers in the city, and I said, "We should do something about this bus system." They just shook their head, "Oh, no, no, no. We can't do anything like that here." So nothing ever came of it. I would carry on my little protests whenever I could.

———————————

I've told people this—when I'm on panels with some of the other folks, they kinda frown at me saying this—but I never intended to be attacked. I did not intend to be anybody's martyr or anything like that. John Lewis and I used to speak together, and John would always say—and he was sincere—"I was prepared to give my life for freedom." And I'm shaking my head. [*Laughs.*]

And I'd say, "No, I was not prepared and did not intend to give my life." So the way I protected myself, if you will—well, first of all, I wasn't as big then as I am now, but I was still taller and bigger than the average person. So if you got one of these thugs out there (one of these cowards I would call it), if they're gonna hit somebody or attack somebody, you got three or four people on the picket line, I would be the last person they would attack. And I always made sure I had the meanest look on my face. And while sometimes they yell and scream at you and you would just kinda look straight ahead or look—I didn't do that. I'd look directly at them. And then pretty soon they would start yelling at the other people. So no, I never intended to be attacked.

When the Freedom Riders reached the bus station in Rock Hill, SC, on May 9th, John Lewis was attacked as soon as he got off the bus. Thomas was next in line to try to achieve the Riders' goal of integrating the station's "white" facilities.

When John Lewis was attacked, it was obvious he could not go into the restroom or the waiting room. It was then my time to get off the bus. And I'm looking at what they're doing to John. Okay. I got up and went to the door of the bus, and I'm there on the front step, and I remember three or four guys right there waiting for me to get off. The door is open and I stood there. And I stared at each one of them.

Miraculously, they moved aside. The look on my face said, "Don't mess with me." They had to think whether or not I'm gonna be nonviolent, okay? They stepped aside and I went into the waiting room. Once again with that mean look on my face. Nobody said anything to me. Of course, then the police came in to arrest me. But I'd perfected that look.

We had our first hunger strike—what was the issue there? I think it was the way the guards addressed us. We wanted them to address us as "Mister" and when they wouldn't people said, "We're going on a hunger strike."

I said, "I don't think that's the way to go because they don't care if we don't eat. That means they're gonna save money."

But I was outvoted. Okay, so we go on this hunger strike. If I'm not mistaken, I may have lasted—some say I only lasted one day. I think I may have lasted three days. But it seemed like a full two or three weeks.

They'd bring the food around. "No, no, I don't want any food." And that third day they brought the food around, I grabbed the tray. And oh my God.

"Hank broke the hunger strike!"

So I ate my food. Then there was total silence. I was being shunned by everybody. Then I got up to make a statement. I said, "The one thing we need in here is strength. We need our strength." [*Laughs.*]

Somebody said I made a hell of a speech, but they all booed me. [*Laughs.*] I said, "We need our strength. And these folks don't care if we die in here. Are we gonna give them that satisfaction?"

I'll never forget after I broke the strike, one of the guys next to me said, "Hank. I'm so glad you did that." [*Laughs.*] But Bernard LaFayette and James Beve, oh, they were hard on me. They were hard on me.

There was an endless parade of politicians coming by to see these Freedom Riders once we were locked up. We had one guy, I've forgotten his name, but when the politicians would come by, he'd jump up on the bars like a monkey and go "Woof, woof, woof."

They also brought school groups. Then something called, I guess, Boys Town or Girls Town—the future lead-

ers of Mississippi. There was always somebody prepared to start talking with the visitors, especially if they were teenagers. One fella I'll never forget was Bill Mahoney. Bill was a very good writer, and he would always have a speech ready to tell 'em what the Freedom Riders was about.

Of course, they were told just to keep moving. But you talked still. To me it was fun. A lot of these kids, the only contacts they had ever had with blacks were the field hands and the maids. So to be able to see blacks who were articulate and could express themselves—even though it was a brief encounter—I'm pretty sure it made some kind of impression on them. ■

DAVID MYERS & WINONAH BEAMER

See page 62

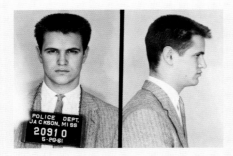

David Myers: I read about the Freedom Ride before it started, about the planning of it. I followed it very closely in the papers. On Mother's Day, May 14, I was home for the weekend in Indiana. That was the day of the Anniston bus burning. I watched that on TV with my parents, and we talked a little bit about it. May 24 was the day of the first arrest in Jackson. When I read about that, it really made me mad that they arrested people who peacefully go in a place and do nothing. The police had chased everybody away, there's no one in there to have any trouble with.

That was the day [David] Fankhauser and I talked about it and I talked to my constitutional law professor, because we had just done *Plessy* vs. *Ferguson* in constitutional law.

Winonah Beamer: I was not involved in activist politics the way David Fankhauser was, from the cradle. I was just responding to things that were going on. First there was the horrible bus burning. Then when I heard there was a way we could get there and something we could actually do, I wanted to go. But David [Myers] and David [Fankhauser] were just kind of—this was their thing, they were keeping it to themselves—

Myers: No, that wasn't what it was. What it was, really, I told you I read about these things all the time. I followed them closely and I knew what the dangers were. I had a feeling from the time I left the campus until I got back in Indiana several weeks later that I might not ever come back alive. At that time I could name you all the lynchings and—Mack Charles

Parker was taken out of the jail he was in and found in the Pearl River tied up with barbed wire. I knew about all those things and I knew that there is no safe place in Mississippi.

Winonah and I had been good friends from the time we met in fall of '59, her first week in college. And one day in March '61 I had a new Leica 500 millimeter lens. I was going out to take some pictures of birds and I was on my Harley-Davidson. I saw Winonah and I said, you want to go with me to the park to take some bird pictures? And she said yes and we started walking down the path and I just reached down and took her hand. And I held her hand and we just walked and walked and we never did take any pictures. And I told her that I had loved her since the first time I had ever seen her and I wanted to marry her. I told her all that that day. So I didn't want her to go to some dangerous place like Mississippi.

Beamer: I wanted to go. And David said no, you can't go. And I said, whoa, whoa, whoa. You're not the boss of me. What is this, I can't go? He and David had by that time met the people and made the contacts and knew how they were gonna get there. And I was excluded.

Myers: David [Fankhauser] and I went around campus collecting money from people. We got in touch with some people at Antioch, where there was a professor, a sociology professor, who knew Martin Luther King and Ralph Abernathy. And he got us in touch with them and some Antioch students drove us to the airport. We flew first to Cincinnati, then

to Atlanta, then to Montgomery. A minister met us at the airport and took us to Abernathy's home on Thursday morning, May 25.

Because of the riots the night before, there were National Guardsmen all around Abernathy's house with machine guns and placements behind sandbags and all that stuff. When we got in the house, seated on the couch watching TV, watching the news, in their pajamas with their plates on their laps eating breakfast, were William Sloane Coffin and Ralph Abernathy and Martin Luther King.

We spent a couple of days there, and then went to Jackson.

Beamer: I went to my mother because I was what, nineteen. And I wanted her to write and sign some kind of release thing that CORE really wanted, especially with young people. And so I was telling mom and my brother, David, another David, came in and he had pictures from *Look* or *Life*, I can't remember which, of the Anniston bombing, with the guy picking his teeth out of his bloody face and the bus burning behind him. And he said, mom, look at this, this is what she's talking about, mom, listen.

And so mother said oh, oh, oh, I don't think so. No. No.

And I said, mother, having gone to all these schools throughout my childhood and with a single-parent mom trying to orchestrate all of this, I have written many excuses and signed your name. I said, mother, either you write it or I'll write it. I've done it before. I can do it again. This isn't gonna make a difference.

So, she did. She finally signed something. I don't know what it was. But it was something that made CORE feel, like, it was a disclaimer if this child doesn't come back, you said it was all right that she could go. So I went down to Jackson, with Pat Bryant and Heath Rush.

Myers: I was in the city jail in Jackson. Heath Rush walked in the day after their arrest and handed me a note from Winonah, saying she was across the street in the county jail. That was the first time I knew she wasn't in Ohio.

Since then, I never told her that she could or couldn't do something.

Most Freedom Riders bailed out at 40 days, which allowed them to preserve their appellate rights. Winonah Beamer decided not to bail out and serve her entire four-month sentence.

Beamer: Some people left early, some people a little later, but they all left. We had more than enough people to do legally, whatever they were going to do. Plus, each person who bailed out cost CORE and not just in terms of money but in terms of effort and time and energy and so on.

With all the comings and goings, it got to feel at times like a supermarket. My feeling was there needed to be a small footnote, what the state of Mississippi was exacting in terms of a punishment for this misdemeanor. This is what it cost Winonah and Pat [Bryant] to go into a waiting room and sit down next to one another.

I think the last Freedom Rider bailed out in late summer or early fall. I stayed in maximum security at Parchman until November—

Myers: She spent September, October, and November as the only female prisoner there in a cell by herself and saw no one except prison guards.

Beamer: Actually, if you don't mind your own company it's not a bad thing.

It was a long row of cells, and I was in the front next to the showers, so when they would let me out to take a shower, twice a week, I would run down to the other end and tag and run back. That was my exercise, because other than that I was in the little cell.

Even though Freedom Riders were not allowed to work in prison, since Sunday was not a work day, the authorities decided that Sundays didn't count against Beamer's sentence.

Beamer: They added up a bunch of Sundays and stuck it on the end. I served December in the county jail in Jackson.

Myers: Winonah was going to be released the day after Christmas. I wanted somebody to be there to greet her when she got out. I didn't have any money. And her mother didn't have any money. She wasn't going down there.

I went to a church I had spoken at earlier, the Trinity CME Church on Martindale Avenue in Indianapolis. And church was just letting out and I told the minister that I wanted to be there when Winonah got out and I didn't have the money. He stopped two of the church elders and took them in his office and they came out and one of them said how much money do you need? I told him what I had, and said another $40 would give me all I need to get me down there and both of us back. He handed me $50.

I went down about two days before Christmas. There was an organization called the Jackson Nonviolent Movement out on Lynch Street. But they had kind of disbanded. I went out

there and knocked and this guy answered the door. He was living in the back room. He was one of the guys that worked with them, and he didn't have anyplace to stay. We slept in easy chairs and on the couch and crawled in and out of windows because we didn't have keys to the door.

The house had a phone that would take incoming calls but you couldn't make outgoing calls. Anyway, Jack [Young, the black attorney in Jackson who represented the Freedom Riders] called me on Christmas morning and told me to get down to the jail right away, Winonah was being released a day early. Took a cab down there; it was a black cab that I got in the black neighborhood, where we were staying. When we got ready to leave the jail, we got a white cab to take us back out there; he didn't want to take us.

Beamer: I was just happy to be out and breathing free air. I had met my goal, I was done. We went to this little place that David spoke of and I got to take a bath for the first time in months. And we took a train back—

Myers: No, Greyhound—

Beamer: We took the Greyhound back. When we finally got to Dayton we took a cab from the Greyhound Station to where my mother was living at the time. And we were, I don't know, about a quarter of a mile away from her house and we were watching the meter and as soon as it hit the thing, David says, stop. And we paid the guy and walked the rest of the way. We didn't have quite enough to get home. ∎

PETER STERLING

See page 69

WE DROVE DOWN TO NEW ORLEANS from Ithaca. Me and [Charles] Haynie and [Joe Henry] Griffith and Paul Greene. We took turns driving.

On the way down I said to myself, "Look, you're about to get married. Buy a steel jockstrap. You gotta protect yourself." So when we got to Louisville, we stopped at a sporting goods store, and everybody bought an aluminum jockstrap. It gave us a little sense of security. We carried it with us to New Orleans and put them on in the morning that we were ready to go into Jackson.

The other thing we did was to—we wore ties, but we were told to sort of slit the tie, in the back, so we couldn't be choked with it. So it would break if somebody tried to yank on it. We did that too.

Also, on the drive down, we knew that when we got into Mississippi, we were going to get stopped. Our car had New York license plates. Joe Griffith was from Texas, and our story was we were going to visit his family.

When we crossed the Mississippi line, Griffith started driving. Sure enough, we got stopped. We weren't speeding, we were just stopped because they saw a New York license plate, but the ruse worked. Griffith got out with his Texas drawl, and said, "Oh, we were just going to visit my mammy and my pappy."

I think the trooper might've asked, "Well, you're not Freedom Riders?" or something like that, and we said, "No, no, no, no." They were definitely looking. ∎

JOHN GAGER

See page 78

CHOPPING COTTON—I REMEMBER that was the threat that was held over us at Parchman. "You better behave yourself. Or we'll put you out there, and you'll have to chop some cotton." We had no idea about what "chopping cotton" meant. Not a clue.

_____

All of us who were active in the civil rights movement, and later in the protests against the war in Vietnam, have wondered where that energy went. Those of us who participated in both phases of protests were convinced, and remain convinced, that we made a difference, that we changed the world in some significant way, that the war in Vietnam came to an end sooner than it would have otherwise.

And there's no question in any of our minds that we really changed the world, not just in the South but in the United States, with respect to civil rights. In *The Strange Career of Jim Crow* by C. Vann Woodward—a great, great book by a Yale historian—Woodward argues that what brought about change wasn't so much about changing the laws as it was about changing patterns of interaction and behavior.

So I wonder sometimes if the biggest effect that we had was for white people in the South to see white folks and black folks just doing stuff together. In fact, white folks following the lead of black folks. Maybe, in the long run, that was the thing that made the biggest impression on people. ∎

MICHAEL AUDAIN

See page 84

THE DAY I LEFT PARCHMAN WAS a very, very interesting day. I checked out around 2:00 or 3:00 in the afternoon. The warden came to see me as I was getting my clothes—taking off my stripes and getting my clothes on, and he said to me, "I got one word of advice for you. You gotta be very careful in the future, because you get more than four of these charges and you'll be up on a habitual criminal charge. And they'll send you away for a long time when you're a habitual criminal."

I said, "Well, sir, I don't really think where I come from, in British Columbia, they're gonna give too much recognition of this offense."

He said "No, son. All them western states, they're all on this habitual criminal thing." [*Laughs.*]

Several months later, I was delighted to see that he was sentenced to a long period in Parchman for embezzling cotton money, from selling the cotton produced at Parchman. Someone sent a clipping from the *New York Times.*

When I left Parchman, they put me in the back of this truck, which was open, with wire all around. I guess I was the only guy going back to Jackson that day. That was the only time I started to get nervous. There was a highway patrol car behind me and one in front, but I said, "Gee, you know, maybe I'm going to get the Ku Klux Klan, or something's going to come after me today."

The truck and the patrol cars all pulled into a roadside place for the guards to have dinner. They went in to eat in this restaurant and I was left all alone outside. I could see them pulling the curtain, peeping at me.

JOAN TRUMPAUER MULLHOLLAND

See page 88

MARV DAVIDOV

See page 96

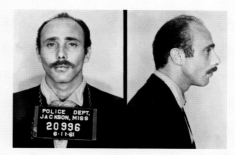

Then townspeople started to come around, to taunt me and throw stuff at me. One guy came with a can and threw it at me and says, "Here's a can of piss for you, you commie."

While that was going on, that's when I saw the guards peeping around the curtain. They could see what was going on. When I got to the jail in Jackson to get released, I was just a mess. I stank.

The deal was, I had to be out of the state by midnight, so my attorney [Jack Young] had to take me to the airport. On the way, we stopped by this house. He said he wanted me to meet this other guy, "a lawyer, a colleague of mine." He said, "This guy wants to shake your hand." It was Medgar Evers.

Evers said, "We read about you in the papers. [*Laughs.*] And we really appreciate what you've done, coming from Canada. We've never had anyone come from Canada before."

When I got home, my father, who was a retired army officer, said I'd made a lot of trouble. He didn't appreciate the publicity I'd had in the Victoria newspapers, and he didn't let me speak to any of the press when I was staying at his house in Victoria. He also had a new wife, too, so that didn't help. [*Laughs.*] ∎

PERIODICALLY, PEOPLE WERE brought into see us in the Hinds County Jail—we were the big attraction.

One day they brought four or five boys, teenagers who were part of Boys State, through for a tour. Our first reaction was laughter, then wisecracks. They got real uneasy. After they went on to other cells, we decided we should be more dignified. When they came back, we sang two verses of "We Shall Overcome," then a pause and a third verse. Someone wolf-whistled and that almost broke us up. But we made it through.

Later when some girls from Girl State were brought through, I made a sign on a piece of paper that read, "I am a Southerner." The jailer took it from me and gave it to one of the girls as a souvenir of her tour. ∎

IN 1961, WE WERE THE BEATS, smoking grass, doing politics. One day at the East Hennepin Bar [in Minneapolis], where we drank, ten people are sitting in the booth and one of them says, "Has everybody slept with everybody else?" We all look around. "Yeah." [*Laughs.*] Smoking grass, fucking each other, doing politics, and dropping out.

One day I hitchhiked from my parents' place to Minneapolis and I'm walking through campus and there's David [Morton] sitting on the steps of a temporary building. We had put out a little magazine together, created buttons—"Hands off Lenny Bruce."

I said, "What's going on?"

"There's a meeting on the Freedom Rides. Come on in." So I go in. Zev [Aelony] had organized it. There were about twelve people there. Zev explains, "This is Wednesday. Friday, we're going to Jackson on a bus. We have money. Who's serious?"

I didn't say anything. He looks at me. "How about you, Marv?"

I said, "I'll tell you by midnight. I'll make up my mind."

I went down to the East Hennepin Bar that night. I told people, "I'm thinking about going on the Freedom Rides on Friday. What do you think?" Everybody said, "One of us should go. It should probably be you." [*Laughs.*]

So next morning I called Zev and said, "Count me in, brother."

On Friday we went down to the Greyhound. There were a lot of media around. There were seven of us who started. When the bus pulled into Madison, Harvey Abrams, a nineteen-year-old Socialist, a deeply involved intellectual, calls his Jewish

MIMI REAL

See page 118

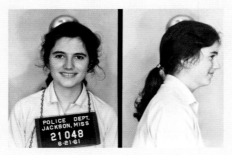

mother. She lays a guilt trip on him and he went home.

I called my Jewish mother. She lays the guilt trip on me, "What are they doing to me now?"

I said, "What do you mean 'they'?"

"Well, this'll kill me."

"Well, Gertie, if this will kill you, I'll make sure you get in the *Guinness Book of Records*. I don't think it'll kill you. I'm going!" *[Laughs.]* ■

I WAS IN A CELL ALL BY MYSELF in the Jackson City Jail, and then I was called into this interrogation room. I honestly did not think that there were people like that sheriff's deputy, or whoever it was who questioned me. He was straight out of central casting, with the accent to boot—literally a red neck, belly hanging over his belt, sitting back in his chair, just totally contemptuous of me.

He asked all the routine questions first. We knew that we were required to give, I think, our name, birth date, Social Security number, and that was it. Anything else, we could refuse to answer, in a very nice way, not in a belligerent way.

Then he started asking me about my personal life. Did I go out with black boys? I'm trying to remember if he asked if I slept with black boys. Then he asked me my religion. CORE had told us that this was a question that was optional but suggested we answer it, simply to show that we weren't godless, atheistic Communists.

You know how you have these mental conversations that you think go on for minutes, but it was obviously only a split second. I thought to myself, "I'm Jewish, but if I say I'm Jewish, I know that, in addition to being racists down here, they're also all a bunch of anti-Semites, so I might get myself into trouble there. But if I say I don't have a religion, or I'm an atheist, or an agnostic, or something, that might be even worse because they're all God-fearing Christians down here. I don't want to be classified as an atheistic, Commie-radical pinko. I could say I was Christian, but that would be lying, and I didn't want to do that."

I finally decided to go with the truth. I figured I was cooked no matter what I said. So I said I was Jewish, at which point he looked at me with this sneer, that only someone in that position could muster, and said, "Oh, so you're a Jewess."

I don't think I had ever heard that term used in conversation. I had certainly seen it. I think Shakespeare, for instance, uses it. It's an archaic term. I had known it in that context, but I had no idea what he even meant. So I don't even think I answered. I was so dumbfounded that I just sat there and looked at him.

Then he said with an equal sneer, "So, you think you're the chosen people. You think you're better than everybody else."

Again, I was totally taken aback. I was so dumbfounded I just didn't say anything.

Mercifully, he went on to the next ridiculous question. I think maybe he wanted to know did I go to school with black boys and stuff like that. But anyway, at some point that was all. He finished his interrogation. ■

MILLER G. GREEN

See page 142

WE WERE AT EL RANCHOS, A PLACE the high school kids frequented after the football games. They had a dancing floor and sold a little beer and food; that was the place to hang out. We were sitting in the booth, talking about who knew. Here comes a man in overalls, which was very unusual. You expected to see a person like that out in the country, at a juke joint. So he politely just made himself comfortable in the booth, and he proceeded to introduce himself. He said his name was James Bevel.

He told us what he and his colleagues were trying to do. At that moment it was like a spirit came over us. We had never seen the man before, and it reminded me of Jesus, when Jesus was walking the earth and how the disciples just picked up and left and didn't tell nobody. That happened to us.

He was not even driving, and this particular night nobody in the group had a car. We thumbed a ride back to where the office was.

When we get there, Tom Gaither, who was a young lawyer and a CORE field secretary, was there. Also Reverend Bevel's wife, Diane Nash, who had just got out of jail that evening. They started to explain what had been going on, what the plan was.

That's when they had asked us to do this task. Several of my friends said, let's wait until tomorrow, we're not clean enough. Well, I knew that that was fear, because we was always clean. I was wearing suits and ties when I was fourteen, fifteen years old, Stacy Adams high-tops. That was basically the attire for my group at the time. So I knew that was fear.

I said, well, if I don't go tonight, I'm not going, and immediately Rev. Bevel and Diane Nash felt that they had a person in the group who was willing. So they continued to talk about what they had been trying to do and what the situation was. And I'm looking at Diane Nash, she was a beautiful girl, and I said to myself, this young lady here just got out of jail and she's beautiful. I said to myself, if she can take a chance, then no reason why I can't go.

So once everybody was in agreement, we were given probably $50, $60 to take a bus to New Orleans. We were told that someone would be there to meet us providing we was able to purchase a ticket through the white interests. After everyone agreed, they dropped us off in front of the Trailway Bus Station. Mind you, I had never seen an African American in there at all. I don't ever remember seeing a black cab driver in there. So now, you are in the process of going into a place that you grew up seeing no blacks in, and you know what the situation is, you know what the rule of law is in the state of Mississippi. I remember getting out just as clear as day, getting out, and I was in front. As I approached the door—and this is so real—there was like a voice that said, "Nigger, you know you ain't got no business going up in here." And there was another voice right after that that said, "Miller, if you even flinch, they're going to run off and leave you, so don't even look back, just keep straight."

———————————

After we were arrested, the police found out we were from Jackson and immediately they told us, you all are from Jackson, we love you all, we know it was that Dr. King that persuaded you all to do this. Get on the phones, call your parents, tell them to come down here and pick you up, everything is all right.

I told the police I was dissatisfied with the way things were, and I said I will be here till the jails rot. We walked around our cells all night. No one was there watching us. They let us have our way. I guess the next morning, probably about 6:30, they recognized that we wasn't going anywhere, and that's when they started fingerprinting us. ■

JESSE HARRIS

See page 144

I DIDN'T UNDERSTAND NONVIOLENCE. I learned all that when we was in Parchman with James Lawson and John Lewis and all of 'em. That's the way we occupied our time. We was engaged in discussions. I was picking up not only the philosophy of nonviolence but history. These people had been active back in the 1950s, in the 1940s. I learned so much.

Before they got there, I think somebody set forth—I think it was James Farmer—said, "Well, this is what we're gonna do. This is the agenda while we're here. We're gonna get up in the morning, make up our bed, say our prayer, and we're gonna start our discussions at 9:00."

I didn't talk about nothing. I was listening. [*Laughs.*] I was loving it. Yeah, was learning it. You could hear it all the way down the hallway. When it was quiet, when no doors slamming and trains rattling and stuff, and you could hear real good. We was laying in the bunk listening to the discussion.

My favorite was Bernard LaFayette, because he was more like the 'hood type, in his conversation. What you call the street talk. He could relate that back to where I came from, to those of us who were from the Jackson area. We could relate to him because he was funny and he was intellectual. Lawson and Farmer, they were talking like they giving a lecture at Harvard University or something, especially when Lawson was talking about the Bible.

When you first go in there, you're fresh. You're wide open. You're fighting for freedom. And you know that you gonna get out. But as time passes, the days—you begin to think,

"Wait a minute, now. Hold it, hold it."

The songs of freedom, that's what would help morale. "Alright, come on. Somebody come out with a song," and that would cheer everybody up. Basically, that's what kept us going, the songs. I was learning new songs. The old spiritual songs—the music's the same but the words have been changed. ■

HEZEKIAH WATKINS

See page 151

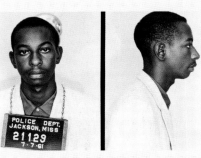

I DON'T WANT TO PUT THE BLAME on nobody, but it seems that these guys here paved the way for a lot—not just blacks, but whites as well. It seems that something needs to be put aside or something needs to be done for them. I can't put it in words, but something is missing.

I have a plate in my head where I was beaten in jail in Jackson [later in the sixties] and sometimes I have severe headaches even now. I tried to use that to get out of the military, but they said, "Hey, he's okay." I just thank the Lord I'm still in my right mind. That's not true for so many people who were in the movement.

I know a lot of the beatings that I received were more severe than what others suffered. But a lot of them was stressed out from their family. The one guy just popped in my mind—he's deceased now, but he had problem with his family. He had problem with the law. After the movement ended, for some reason he couldn't get back on track, and he ended up being in trouble with the police. He couldn't find a job. I think he got picked up a few times for breaking and entering, and the next thing I know, he was dead. I'm told it was natural causes. This happened to quite a few of us.

I don't know this guy's name, but two weeks ago he was brought by the store by another veteran, and I tried very hard to remember him. He said he vaguely remembered me. He's just a little older than I am, but his mind is gone. I asked the guy who brought him by, "What wrong with him?" He said, "He been like that, man, been like that." You just shake your head. ■

LARRY BELL

See page 156

ONE OF THE GUARDS AT PARCHMAN was named Sergeant Story; he was an older man. Deputy sheriff Tyson, he had that drooling, bigoted look. He looked at you from under his brow and snarled. Sergeant Story was an older, gray-haired man, but Deputy sheriff Tyson was the one who ran the whole situation. Everybody jumped when he spoke. He had his cigar and he had a flat top; he was the Class-A Marine. If you look at one of these movies where the old sheriff got his cigar hanging out of his mouth and has his attitude—he drooled with kind of like a picture of dislike and hatred.

Once they took our clothes away as punishment. We protested by singing "We Shall Overcome" and the old Freedom Rider songs. That got them to a point they were going to teach us, so they opened up the windows and let the mosquitoes in. They turned the air conditioning off during the day and so we burned up during the day; and at night when it got cool, they turned the air conditioning on when we were trying to sleep, and we pretty much froze.

About once or twice a week, we were allowed to take a shower. And we all had to shave with one razor— a single-edge razor blade. Now, that was torture in itself! [*Laughs.*] I don't appreciate the Gillette Company too much right now for that. I think we had two minutes to get our showers done, and we got back to our cells.

We had three meals per day, if you want to call them meals. In the morning, they would bring us some cold grits and something that was supposed to be a biscuit. Sometimes we would get a piece of what was supposed to be bacon, but it was fat-

back, really. It was real salty. The grits were—you could pick it up and break it and do whatever you want. Sometimes they'd bring cold oatmeal the same way. It was really curdled up, but hey, we ate it. Didn't have anything else to eat. Didn't have any kind of facilities in our cells where we could prepare anything. We didn't get very much vegetables, so we lost a lot of weight. I lost a lot of weight, and being just kept inside, we were not allowed to go out and didn't get any exposure to the sun, so I lost all of the coloration. It was something. It was an experience.

We were protesting one night, and the next thing, Sergeant Story, he calls Deputy Tyson out; and Deputy Tyson opened up the cells and put all of us— there was a whole side, I guess maybe about thirty-five—put us not in solitary confinement but in the box. It was one room that was smaller than twelve by twelve. They stuck all of us in there.

This is when I think we came closest to someone's demise. When they put us in this lock-up, it was airtight as it was, at least they believed it was airtight. There was no windows; it was just a dark room. So they put all of us in that room, and all we could do is stand up, stand up straight. And it got so hot in there that water was dripping from the ceiling down on us, enough to get us wet.

That's why we were put into the lock-up. They was gonna make us concede to their power, and we refused to concede to their power. Story came up; he opened up the [hole in the door] and said, "Before you get out of here, every damn one of you niggas is gonna tell me 'yes, sir.' "

We said, "Well, why should we tell you 'yes, sir'? We have no disrespect or respect for you. You're a man just like we are."

We were breathing 'cause we thought, "Well, hey, everything is fine. We can stand up in here. As long as we're packed in here like this like sardines, that's no problem." And then we heard, "DUUUUUUuuuuu." The air conditioning was going off. Some individuals started getting concerned, and I noticed that there was a crack at the bottom of the door, because you could see a slit of light there. So I worked my way down and got close to the floor, so here I am, I'm breathing good air! After a while, my comrades began to panic and I thought, "let me tell these guys the secret." So we took turns up and down to get what air we could get.

And when Deputy Tyson came back in and they opened up the little hole on the door, and Sergeant Story, he looked in and we were all dripping wet, he said, "All you niggas shined your ass this time, didn't you?"

"The condition is every one of you niggers—when I ask you a question," he says, "I want everybody to say, 'yes, sir,' to respect my authority.

"Or else your ass is gonna stay in there and you're gonna die."

So some of us acknowledged "yes, sir," and some of us didn't. But they opened the door and let us out, because I don't know if they wanted to have the scandal [of having a Freedom Rider die].

We had an opportunity to share a lot about the movement in Parchman. We had debates, pro and con about race relationships, about segregation. My

BILL SVANOE

See page 172

brother-in-law [Edmond Dalbert] was the pro and I was the con. He put up the defense for the whites, and I debated him from the standpoint of the blacks. We went over a myriad of topics. He wanted to know, "Well, I'm white. Why should I give you what I have and thereby compromise myself?"

It wasn't just a casual conversation; it was to bring some kind of a resolve or strong thinking to the issues. After he and I got through, we asked "OK, who do you think was strongest?" and everybody would respond by clapping.

Believe it or not, the officials of the prison would come and listen to us debate. Tyson and Story, they'd be there listening to us debating. Did it have any effect on them? We didn't see any change, they didn't express any change. But the fact that it was being listened to and that applause was given—and sure, it was the cellmates and everything—but where they were positioned, they listened to the debate and didn't interrupt. ∎

WE WERE ON THE BUS TO JACKSON, and we were supposed to maintain a low profile, not let anybody know we were Freedom Riders. There were like, nine or ten of us on this bus, which was crowded with other people. This one Rider, I can't remember his name, he started talking about the fact that we were Freedom Riders.

I was sitting next to this drunk ex-Marine—big guy, my size, older guy, and he got really angry about it. He said, "You guys, you're trying to upset things! Leave these niggers alone!" He just went on and on, and he started getting really angry, and he pulls a loaded 45mm automatic. I happen to know because I was on the rifle team when I was in ROTC. He said, "You know, I could blow you all away right now. I could blow you away!" And he puts the gun to my head.

Fortunately, my mother was an alcoholic, and so were my uncles. I knew how to deal with mean drunks. I knew job No. 1 was to get him to quiet down, because things flare up, and then they go down, they flare up again. If I could just get him to calm down, maybe something would work out.

I slowly talked this guy down. He was really on the edge of something. He was drunk, and he was angry, and he was mean as can be, and he had a loaded gun, and of course, the whole bus was like, "Ah!" Everybody was trying to pretend it wasn't happening, but everybody saw it.

I don't remember what I said, but I just kept talking. He finally put the gun away and just sort of mumbled. But this one Rider kept trying to engage him, which really pissed me off. I'm pretty good in emergencies,

but I kept thinking about could I get the gun away from him? Would somebody else be hurt? All that stuff, but I felt the best way was to talk him out of it.

The bus driver was a big burly guy. When he found out we were Freedom Riders, he was really pissed. He made an unscheduled stop: "Oh, we're doing a rest stop." People were exiting the bus in no time.

When the ex-Marine got off the bus, there were cops there to arrest him. The bus driver pulls me aside, and he said, "Listen, I don't agree with what you are doing here. But that was too much."

So the bus driver essentially handled it. I'll never forget that, because it was a real human moment. He didn't like what we were doing. He didn't believe in it, but he still knew that this was over the top. ∎

PAUL BREINES
See page 184

HERMAN TARNOWER WAS MY mother's cardiologist. He didn't have any diet stuff with her, but he was my mother's cardiologist. When I got home from Mississippi, she said, "I made an appointment with Dr. Tarnower. You need a thorough physical." I remember him putting his hands on my balls and saying, "Now would you look away while I examine your genitalia?" Then I went back to Wisconsin.

I gave a talk, as a returned Freedom Rider. I was feeling like—it was this thing that has been with me since. I was so blown away by meeting people who were on the Freedom Rides who were from Jackson, and just thinking like, "When these people get out, they're not going back to Herman Tarnower to have their genitals examined. They're not gonna have their genitals examined probably. Who knows what access they have to medical care? Not only that, what are they living in?"

Especially after Ray Arsenault's book came out, I got emails and letters from people saying, "Oh, my God. I forgot that you had been on the Freedom Rides," or "I had no idea you did this. That's so great." I appreciate that, but it doesn't feel that way to me.

People have actually said to me, "Can't you just take more credit?" I get teary. I think, "No. I know it seems weird to you, like false modesty and stuff, but you can't imagine what an impression it made to realize I live this totally privileged life. I risked my life—I understand that. But compared to what people who came from Mississippi and Georgia and Louisiana, who were doing this, I feel so humbled."

I'm still a political person. About five years ago I started to pick up trash in my neighborhood. I go around once or twice a day. It's great exercise. I take a little plastic bag, I have heavy gloves and I pick shit up in a route here. People in the neighborhood know me. Someone made me a sweatshirt that says White Trash Collector.

This is the sort of feeling I had when I went on the Freedom Ride. I thought, "We can change the world." I still think I can change the world, but it takes the form of keeping my neighborhood clean, and just going around and picking up trash. It's not as historic. It's completely individual. It comes out of despair. It comes out of thinking, you know, what is enlightened politics? I know what it is, but it doesn't exist. So I pick up trash. I don't have an illusion that it's politically valuable, but I do have the feeling that it keeps the neighborhood clean. ∎

RICHARD STEWARD
See page 214

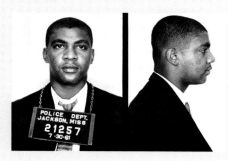

WHEN WE WERE RELEASED FROM Parchman, we were given our clothes and whatever belongings we had, in paper sacks. I notice that this officer was watching me. He just had his eyes on me and I knew who he was 'cause I heard about his infamy.

So that guy said, "Where's your's?"
I said, "Right there, over there."
So he went to pick it up—his name was Sergeant Story—and came over to me. He said, "Is this yours?"
And I said, "Yeah."
He said, "Yeah, what?"
I said, "Yeah, it's mine."
He said, "Yes, what?"
I said, "Yeah, officer of the law. That's mine."
He said, "Look, boy. Your ass hasn't left here yet."

Right at that moment, I thought, "This motherfucker gonna put me in this shit with the real deal." Like he brought the reality back to me.
I said, "Yes, sir. That's my bag."
"All right. Now get your ass on outta here."

Whew! But I hated it. I hated to do that but I felt like there was no choice. I gotta get outta here. That was one that will stay with me the rest of my life. ∎

FREEDOM RIDER INDEX

ACKNOWLEDGMENTS

My thanks above all to the Freedom Riders whom I have met and photographed, for their willingness to share their stories and their time.

Thanks also to the Freedom Riders who shared their archival materials: the newspaper photograph on pages 2-3 is courtesy of Jorgia Siegel as are the CORE hat and button on page 23; the mass-meeting poster on page 218 is courtesy of Daniel Stevens; the chess set on page 240, made from bread in Parchman by Byron Baer, is courtesy of Robert Rogers, who spirited it out of prison.

Thanks to everyone at the Mississippi Department of Archives and History, especially Sarah Morrow, who guided me through the State Sovereignty Commission files. Thanks also to Dave Pilcher, Celia Tisdale, Matthew Glover, and Chrissy Wilson.

The comments by Helen and Bob Singleton, on pages 210 and 213, are from oral histories made for *The Children Shall Lead*, a documentary on the Freedom Rides produced by the William Winter Institute for Racial Reconciliation at the University of Mississippi. All other comments by the Freedom Riders are from the interviews I conducted with them.

Apart from being an excellent history, Ray Arsenault's *Freedom Riders: 1961 and the Struggle for Racial Justice* (Oxford, 2006) was a great aide in helping locate Riders.

James Atlas and the folks at Atlas saw the possibilities of this project early on, when it was more idea than reality. *Breach of Peace* became a reality thanks to the generous enthusiasm of Karen Pritzker.

Thanks go to many friends and colleagues: Carmen Lewis; Elise Pittman; Eric McClellan; Michael Schnetzer; Lindsey David; Marie Elena Scaturro; Paul Christopher Dowd; Brendan Fitzgibbons; Jan Hillegas; William Ashley Vaughan; Julian Cox; Amadon Diallo; Jamie Pallot; Robert N. Solomon; Gerry Marzaroti; Kathy Ryan; Pat Towers; Shelby Lee Adams; Bruce Fraser; Susan Glisson; April Grayson; Kevin McDermott; Suzanne and Robert Sullivan; Vanessa Cho and Matthew Simmons; Isaac Pollan; Judith Belzer; and Michael Pollan; and Will Dana.

Finally, thanks to my parents, Nora and Tam Etheridge, and my sister, Anne, and her partner, Robert Porter. I can't imagine having done this without Kate Browne, my wife, or Maud, our daughter. Kate's ideas about how to execute this project have been invaluable; her judgments are reflected everywhere in these pages.

CREDITS

Page 1: Clip from the Jackson *Clarion-Ledger* from the State Sovereignty Commission files, courtesy of the Mississippi Department of Archives & History (MDAH). SCRID # 2-140-1-281-1-1-1.

Pages 2-3: Photograph courtesy of Jorgia Siegel, arrested June 20.

Pages 4-5: © Bettmann/Corbis

Page 6: © Hulton Archive /Getty Images Photo by William Lovelace

Page 7: © Bettmann/Corbis

Pages 8-9, 10-11: All courtesy of the MDAH. These images were created from 16mm film news footage shot by a local TV station. Page 8: MP 1980.01: WLBT Newsfilm Collection Reel D9 Item 38-1. Page 9: MP 1980.01: WLBT Newsfiilm Collection Reel D9 Item 38-2. Page 10: MP 1980.01: WLBT Newsfilm Collection Reel D9 Item 47.

Page 23: Hat and button courtesy of Jorgia Siegel.

Pages 28-29: State Sovereignty Commission memo courtesy of the MDAH. SCRID #2-55-2-66-1-1-1 (page 28) and 2-55-2-66-2-1-1 (page 29).

Page 31 and following: All mug shots are from the State Sovereignty Commission files and courtesy of the MDAH. All mug shots are online and can be searched at: www.mdah.state.ms.us/bugle/sovcom/

The originals were scanned by archivists at the MDAH. I have cleaned up the images, removing dust and spots, but not retouching staple marks, punch holes or light leaks. I also sharpened the images and increased contrast.

Page 218: Poster courtesy of Daniel Stevens, arrested July 7.

All other photographs are by Eric Etheridge.

AUTHORS

Eric Etheridge was born in 1957. He grew up in Carthage and Jackson, Mississippi, and is a graduate of Vanderbilt University. He has worked as an editor at a number of magazines, including *Rolling Stone, 7 Days,* the *New York Observer,* and *Harper's* magazine. He as also worked online, creating and running websites for Microsoft, the *New York Times,* and others. He lives in New York City with his wife, Kate Browne, and their daughter, Maud.

Roger Wilkins is a Pulitzer Prize-winning journalist and distinguished professor of history at George Mason University. He was assistant attorney general in President Lyndon B. Johnson's administration at the age of thirty-three.

Diane McWhorter is the Pulitzer Prize-winning author of *Carry Me Home: Birmingham, Alabama—the Climactic Battle of the Civil Rights Revolution* and a long-time contributor to the *New York Times.*

BREACH OF PEACE

**PORTRAITS OF THE
1961 MISSISSIPPI FREEDOM RIDERS**

By Eric Etheridge
Preface by Roger Wilkins
Foreword by Diane McWhorter

Copyright © 2008 by Eric Etheridge
Preface copyright © 2008 by Roger Wilkins
Foreword copyright © 2008 by Diane McWhorter

Design by Giampietro+Smith

For more information about the Breach of Peace project, please visit www.breachofpeace.com.

Atlas & Co. *Publishers*
15 West 26th Street, 2nd floor
New York, NY 10010
www.atlasandco.com

Distributed to the trade by W. W. Norton & Company

Grateful acknowledgment is made to Karen Pritzker for her support on this project.

Atlas & Company books may be purchased for educational, business, or sales promotional use. For information, please write to info@atlasandco.com.

Library of Congress Cataloging-in-Publication Data is available upon request.
Printed in China
ISBN-13: 978-0-9777433-9-1
13 12 11 10 09 08   1 2 3 4 5 6

For Kate

CHESS SET

Chess pieces made from bread by Byron Baer (see page 198) in Parchman. The pieces were smuggled out of Parchman by Robert Rogers (see page 160).